The Work of Friendship

SUNY series in the Philosophy of the Social Sciences
Lenore Langsdorf, editor

The Work of Friendship

·

Rorty, His Critics, and the
Project of Solidarity

Dianne Rothleder

State University of New York Press

Published by
State University of New York Press, Albany

© 1999 State University of New York

For information, address State University of New York Press,
State University Plaza, Albany, NY, 12246

Production by Dale Cotton
Marketing by Patrick Durocher

Library of Congress Cataloging-in-Publication Data

Rothleder, Dianne, 1964–
    The work of friendship : Rorty, his critics, and the project of
solidarity / Dianne Rothleder.
        p.   cm. — (SUNY series in the philosophy of the social
sciences)
    Includes bibliographical references and index.
    ISBN 0-7914-4127-X (hc : alk. paper). — ISBN 0-7914-4128-8 (pbk.
: alk. paper)
    1. Rorty, Richard. 2. Friendship. I. Title. II. Series.
B945.R524R68   1999
191—dc21   98-8132
                                                        CIP

10 9 8 7 6 5 4 3 2 1

For Friends

Contents

•

Acknowledgments

●

When a project has stretched out over several years, the number of people who have offered support grows proportionately. More than one city, more than one editor, and even a new member of the family have all played a role in the writing of this book.

Since there is no discernable natural starting point for this book and for the support I've had, I'll devise an artificial one. I'd like to thank Susan Moller Okin who was my first political theory teacher. She gave me questions that have resonated with me ever since my first year of college at Brandeis University.

Andrée Collard, another teacher, gave me the twin gifts of feminism and activism, which could channel anger into creativity and frustration into outreach.

The first draft of this book was written with the support of a marvelous group of new mothers who had to contend with old lives, new lives, and new life all at once. Our weekly get-togethers started out as escape from isolation and ended up as committed friendship. Mary Harms and Christopher, Marcy Kovas and Katie, Ann Graham Price and Katie, and Judith Robert and Sophia—the mothers are all strong women who helped me learn about friendship and strength and separation, and the children helped me learn about play. Welcome to Clay, Caroline, Michael, Emily, and Fiona.

Moving meant starting over. Luckily Amy Cuthbert and Talia Gordon were at the park on the right day. Amy's down-to-earth voice has helped enormously as I have revised my work. Sandra Hellestrae and Michelle Mowery have been friends, mothers, and counselors at all the right times.

Nathan Tarcov, Stephen Holmes, Arnold Davidson, and Robert Pippen offered their time and comments on an earlier version. David Hall, Cynthia Willett, and an anonymous reader read and commented extensively and though I did not take all of their suggestions, their voices can certainly be found here.

Alison Brown, Ann Clark, Carol Denson, Carmela Epright, Laura Hengehold, Dan Price, and Mike Washburn all offered support and ideas at various times over the years.

My editors Clay Morgan, Priscilla Ross, and Jane F. Bunker have seen this project turn from a manuscript into a book, and though they do this routinely, they did not make me feel like part of their routine.

My family of origin helped with support and patience and listened to my fusses.

My daughter Megan Rose and my son Quinn Elliott have given me the gift of play. Whether with food, blocks, or words, these children are creativity itself. Megan, at six, already writes books, and Quinn, at sixteen months, eats them, and says "read it."

My husband, Andrew Cutrofello, has provided support beyond belief. He types, he heats up frozen pizzas almost as well as I do, he plays with children, he hugs, he listens. He is a friend.

Jacques Derrida, "Biodegradables," in *Critical Inquiry,* Vol. 15 #4, Summer 1989, © 1989 by The University of Chicago Press. Reprinted by permission of The University of Chicago Press.

John McCumber, "Reconnecting Rorty: The Situation of Discourse in Richard Rorty's *Contingency, Irony, and Solidarity*" in *Diacritics,* Summer 1990 © by The Johns Hopkins University Press. Reprinted by permission of the Johns Hopkins University Press.

Richard Rorty, *Contingency, Irony, and Solidarity* © 1989 by Cambridge University Press. Reprinted by permission of Cambridge University Press.

Richard Rorty, *Philosophy and the Mirror of Nature,* © 1979 by Princeton University Press. Reprinted by permission of Princeton University Press.

"Trotsky and the Wild Orchids" by Richard Rorty, from *Wild Orchids and Trotsky* by Mark Edmundson, editor. Copyright © 1993 by Mark Edmundson. Used by permission of Viking Penguin, a division of Penguin Putnam Inc.

Introduction

•

The primary focus of this work is Richard Rorty's "firm distinction between the public and the private." The argument I offer is, first, that Rorty's distinction has its roots in his take on epistemology, in his autobiography, and in his political theory; second, that this distinction—at least as Rorty casts it—is untenable; and third, that Rorty's tenacious hold on this distinction undermines what he takes to be the most central ethical concern—cruelty, and more specifically, humiliation. The final sections of this work are given over to discussing a notion of friendship that both transcends the public/ private distinction and makes humiliation impossible. The discussion of friendship draws on Lyotard's notion of the *différend*, Habermas's work on communication, and Derrida's work on the gift.

Chapter 1, "Analytic Rorty, Psychoanalytic Theory, and the Question of the Other," shows how Rorty's political concerns are entwined with his take on epistemology. For Rorty, foundational truth and grounded certainty give way to conversational agreement—capital-T Truth becomes small-t truth. This development is directly related to the social because truth ceases to be an epistemological issue and becomes instead a social one.

Because truth is social for Rorty, the truths of the political arena must be watered-down, must be platitudinous so that there can be the same kind of broad consensus that epistemology aims at. (The platitudinous nature of Rorty's political sphere is taken up more in the section of Chapter 4 entitled "Communication and the *Différend.*")

Another link between Rorty's epistemological stance and his political theory comes from his doing away with privileged access as an epistemological phenomenon. Without the real privacy of the mental that privileged access sets up, there is no real privacy. But Rorty's account of irony requires that there be a private sphere. Since the private cannot be a mentalist notion, it becomes a political notion. The public/private distinction, then, shifts from the epistemic to the problems with Rorty's public/private distinction.

The conclusion of *Philosophy and the Mirror of Nature* is an argument for the practice of hermeneutics. I argue in chapter 1 that Rorty's hermeneutic approach is a structurally modest and therefore antiradical position. If hermeneutics is what is to replace epistemology, then liberal, reformist politics must win out over radical change. I conclude the chapter by showing how Rorty's work is suffused with antiradicalism from his account of hermeneutics to his discussion of vocabulary shifts, from his genius model of historical change to his emphasis on reading/consuming rather than on writing/poesis.

Chapter 2, "Possible Worlds and Narrative Convention," discusses Rorty's account of reading and redescribing. Because redescription is, for Rorty, an exercise in cruelty and humiliation, I turn to Artaud whose work on the theater of cruelty is the best explication of the cruel desire for the originary. This chapter takes the private sphere's viewpoint to show why the private must, on Rorty's account, be separate from the public. It also refines the discussion of antiradicalism from the first chapter.

Chapter 3, "Negative Solidarity," discusses Rorty's notion of solidarity as a public phenomenon that is kept far from private concerns. The touchstone of the chapter is Rorty's autobiographical essay "Trotsky and the Wild Orchids," and the basic

thrust of the argument is that Rorty's public/private distinction
has a strong autobiographical grounding.

The first three chapters, then, ground Rorty's public/
private distinction and show why it is that he feels he needs it.
Chapter 4, "In Between Circus Freaks and Dead Fathers," questions the tenability of this distinction. Each section of the chapter offers a reading of the first three sentences of Harold Bloom's
Anxiety of Influence from a different perspective. And each reading shows one or more problems with Rorty's public/private
distinction.

The first reading, "Dialectics," is from a Hegelian perspective. I argue that the strong poet can be located early on in the
Phenomenology, and that this position is, therefore, unstable. The
Hegelian reading suggests that Rorty needs dialectical movement rather than reified stasis.

The second reading, "Care," is a Rortian critique of Rorty in
that Rorty retains a notion of care that somehow disappears when
he takes on the persona of the strong poet. I argue that Rorty
should stick to a notion of care and that, in any event, the
originary position for which the strong poet strives can be seen
as illusory once creation is properly understood.

The third reading, "The Personal and the Political," discusses Sandra Lee Bartky's essay, "Feminine Masochism and the
Politics of Personal Transformation." I argue that by trying to
insulate the personal from political judgments, Rorty not only
loses a valuable source of social critique, but also loses sight of
the real political issues involved in identity-formation.

The fourth reading, "The Paradox of Recognition," discusses
Derrida's work on the gift as it relates to Rorty's desire for a well-
defined, reified space for transgression. The paradox of the gift
is that once a gift is recognized as such, it joins the circle of
economic obligation and hence ceases to be a gift. But if the gift
is not recognized as a gift, then still it is not a gift. This paradox
is generalized to all forms of recognition, and hence to all distinctions that must be recognized. Because the dividing line
between the public and the private is so crucial for Rorty's
account, it is a line that must be recognized; but the logic of

this paradox suggests that it cannot be recognized without being simultaneously annihilated.

The fifth and final section of chapter four, "Communication and the *Différend*," focuses on the Habermas/Rorty debate
and on the Habermas/Lyotard debate.

Habermas wishes to preserve a regulative notion of reason.
Reason is tripartite—reflecting the post-Kantian split between
the true (scientific reason), the good (moral reason), and the
beautiful (aesthetic reason). For Habermas, each of these domains has a logic and a discourse, and each must critique itself
and the other two. Each has an unrealized ideal that grounds
critique and allows us to render judgment and preserve some
notion of progress.

Rorty rejects Habermas's work on this for two related reasons. First, Rorty has no truck with transcendent reason; and
second Rorty wants an aesthetic sphere (the private) that is
immune to any political or truth-concerned judgment. What
guides Rorty's private sphere is solely the aesthetic, and any
concern for others or for getting things right interferes with the
Romantic, originary strong poet side of Rorty.

Within the public sphere, the moral and the scientific lose
much of their efficacy and worth because Rorty's peculiar construction of the public as a place of platitudes leaves little space
for real difference and substantive debate. Rorty argues that
liberal political institutions may need some gradual tinkering,
but that they are basically doing what needs to be done and so
no one need be concerned about the public sphere.

By doing away with what he calls "Capital-T Truths," Rorty
weakens the force of Truth claims within the public sphere; and
by arguing that the most substantive moral category is that of
cruelty, Rorty seemingly settles all of our ethical differences as
well. With the concerns of the public sphere dealt with before
the conversation gets going, Rorty has made discussions of public
matters seemingly unnecessary.

It is this "seemingly" that Lyotard's work on the *différend*
helps to clarify. The *différend* is a structural silence that cannot

be spoken without self-annihilation and so is not spoken and hence is not recognized. Because the pain of the *différend* is passed over in silence, it *seems* that all's right with the world, when in fact there is much that is terribly wrong.

Chapter 5 "Friendships of Play," parallels chapter four in structure. This chapter, then, is a close reading of educator Vivian Gussin Paley's phrase "You can't say you can't play," which is the title of one of her books, and is also the rule she instituted in her kindergarten class.

This phrase is interpreted first through the works of Luce Irigaray to offer an Irigarayan critique of exclusion and inclusion in the theory and practice of psychoanalysis. I then turn again to Derrida's writings on the "de Man affair" to help illustrate the responsibilities inherent in friendships. Next, Aristotle provides a counterexample with his insistence on exclusionary, and in a sense easy, friendships. I then turn to radical educator Herbert Kohl and to Lyotard to show the problems with inclusion. Some people refuse inclusion, and some people cannot be included without self-annihilation. I conclude the chapter and the book with a discussion of Rorty's irony and I suggest that we need a positive basis for solidarity—laughter and friendship, rather than Rorty's negative basis—collective fear of humiliation.

CHAPTER ONE

Analytic Rorty, Psychoanalytic Theory,

and the Question of

the Other

This chapter has two aims that will help develop my overarching theory of friendship. First I want to look at Rorty's take on analytic philosophy, his debunking of the epistemic project and show that this position not only underlies his public/private distinction, but also sets up a notion of otherness that makes friendship more difficult. Second, I want to show that his reading of the history of philosophy puts him in the position of psychoanalyst. Rorty the analyst uses the history of philosophy as an other, I argue; from this viewpoint, Rorty's treatment of others can again be elucidated.

For Rorty, the question of whether "I am in pain" refers to a mental state or to a material state is both uninteresting and wrongheaded. He develops his discussion of the Antipodeans in *Philosophy and the Mirror of Nature* to show this. What I find interesting about his discussion is first that it centers on pain, and second, that he creates a fictive other to illustrate a very different, but in the end, not very different, way of conceptualizing and conveying pain.

Pain is the thing in others that Rorty would have us respond to in his notion of solidarity. In *Contingency, Irony, and Solidarity*, the emphasis on pain shifts to the psychic pain of

1

humiliation, while in *Philosophy and the Mirror of Nature* the pain seems to be physical.

In both cases, other people's pain can elicit from someone a variety of responses. One can believe or disbelieve the pain based on the behavior of the person in pain. Because the pain is in someone else, one acts based on a judgment about behavior rather than on direct knowledge of the pain. Pain, then, acts to separate us into nonintersubjective beings. I will recognize your pain only if I recognize you as being capable of feeling pain and only if I recognize your pain behavior as such.

If one chooses to believe the pain, and further, to empathize with the person in pain, then pain functions as a basis for unity. Indeed, in *Contingency*, Rorty's notion of solidarity rests primarily on empathizing with pain.

Because Rorty would have us make judgments about the validity of pain claims, he privileges pain over other potentially more intersubjective experiences. What seems to result is a parading of pain—not unlike what is on daytime television talk shows—in an attempt to elicit empathy. If each pain and pained subject must stand for judgment, then we end up with pain as spectacle (television news and talk shows), boredom over other people's pain (disaster burnout), and a ratcheting up of intensity to combat the boredom (talk shows leading eventually to a murder).

Because, for Rorty, we gain access to the other through pain—something we do not have access to, the other is in the position of having to prove him-/her-/itself to us. The act of proving pain becomes a major form of social entertainment whether through Rorty's novels, or through television, or sports. The role of entertainer is both racially and class charged, and instead of rescuing us from this system, Rorty bolsters it by using pain as the basis for solidarity.

The important question at this point is what if analytic Rorty decided not to use a discussion of pain to show that the materialist Antipodeans were just like the mentalist terrestrials?

What if solidarity with the Antipodeans had nothing to do with the fact that though they seem different, they are not really so different after all? What if it did not matter to the terrestrials whether or not they could or did feel pain? What if the Antipodeans were irreducibly different? Really other?

It would seem, within Rorty's account, that we would treat the Antipodeans the way we treat all the other others—we would enslave them or eat them or fight a war with them to gain access to their resources. For Rorty, our response to otherness is based on our judgment of the worth of the other. The other is worth more if seen to be like us, and worthless if seen to be different. Rorty's liberalism tempers this because he hopes that we will accept more and more others as like us over time, but this acceptance is, again, based on their proving their worth to us.

By deprivileging privileged access, Rorty seemingly reduces the importance of the other's experience and voice. It is not interesting for him that someone's pain is felt more by that someone than by an observer and so there is less room in this account for the other to speak. Although Rorty later argues that novels and narratives are important sources of information for developing empathy, his epistemic position undermines both the need to tell one's story and the effect that stories have on readers. If privileged access is not so privileged, then other people's stories are not so important.

The anti-epistemic position has another major effect on Rorty's later writings, I would argue. Doing away with the notion of privileged, private mentalist experience forces Rorty to re-create some kind of private space elsewhere. This he does in his "firm distinction" between the public and the private. The unreachable unspeakable mental gives way to the unviewable and unjudgable living room with the shades drawn and the phone unplugged.

What this step does is to move solipsism from inside the head, as it were, to inside the house. Rorty's subject knows that there is a public sphere elsewhere but she exists mainly in the private space of reading and fantasizing at home. Ironically, though, the private ironist is not to speak publicly of her private thoughts and so not only does Rorty's public/private distinction re-create privileged access, it also re-creates the unspeakable of epistemology.

The difference with Rorty's move is that his unspeakable is so because of shame and fear, while the unspeakable for epistemology is so because of the structural limits of language and knowledge. Rorty's unspeakable leads to self-silencing, isolation and depression because it is negatively imposed on each subject; while epistemology's unspeakable, at worst, leads to bad philosophy or bad poetry. *Philosophy and the Mirror of Nature* clearly is a sustained argument against bad philosophy, but it is also in effect an argument against depression. Dr. Rorty's diagnosis is that philosophy is suffering from bipolar mood disorder, and his therapeutic prescription is that philosophy give up on its dreams of grandeur and consequently on its nihilistic reactions as well. Philosophy and politics, too, must learn to be content in a modest middle.

In *Philosophy and the Mirror of Nature*, Rorty identifies Wittgenstein, Heidegger, and Dewey as the most important philosophers of the twentieth century. Each of these thinkers is important, for Rorty, because each overcame his youthful desire to make philosophy foundational, and moved instead toward therapy and edification (Rorty 1979, 5).

In many discussions of Rorty's work, there are references to dualisms, dichotomies, poles, and splits, and the concomitant therapeutic prescriptions for healing and overcoming. Rorty, hearkening back to Wittgenstein, talks about philosophy as therapy. Given all this language about polar opposites and healing, it might well be worthwhile to characterize Rorty's version of the history of philosophy as a diagnosis of bipolar mood disorder, which used to be called manic-depressive disorder.[1]

In philosophy's manic phases, thinkers attempt to provide foundations for all thought and all existence. There is this giddy feeling that everything can be accounted for, can be placed, and can be systematized. But "reality" sinks in, seeming failures abound, and the mood rapidly shifts to the depressive phase in which nihilism abounds. Nothing can be said, there are no generalizations, no commonalities. Systematic philosophy is a grand failure, a delusion. Giddiness turns morose, and we are all abandoned, isolated, and suicidal.

In characterizing the early manic projects of his three heroes, Rorty writes:

> Wittgenstein tried to construct a new theory of representation which would have nothing to do with mentalism, Heidegger to construct a new set of philosophical categories which would have nothing to do with science, epistemology, or the Cartesian quest for certainty, and Dewey to construct a naturalized version of Hegel's vision of history. (Rorty 1979, 5)

In each case, Rorty chooses language that makes these projects look grandiose. If these projects were Hollywood film treatments, they would never receive financial backing from any sane studio heads. And were they to be filmed, they would certainly be bigger flops than was *Heaven's Gate*.

In showing that the three overcame their youthful mania, Rorty writes:

> Each of the three came to see his earlier effort as self-deceptive, as an attempt to retain a certain conception of philosophy after the notions needed to flesh out that conception (the seventeenth-century notions of knowledge and mind) had been discarded. (Rorty 1979, 5)

The three heroes, then, were self-deceptive in that they were not attuned to the fact that their positions were unsupportable. Worse yet, the supports they needed dated from the seventeenth century. If the seventeenth century is the dawn of modernity, the infancy of science, then to hearken back to that time is to regress to infancy. Perhaps such regression is allowable for youthful work, but a mature philosopher ought really to overcome infantile desires.[2]

Rorty continues:

> Each of the three, in his later work, broke free of the Kantian conception of philosophy as foundational, and spent time warning us against those very temptations to which he himself had once succumbed. Thus their later work is therapeutic rather than constructive, edifying rather than systematic, designed to make the reader question his own motives for philosophizing rather than to supply him with a new philosophical program. (Rorty 1979, 5–6)

Rorty's choice of metaphor here is curious. There is liberation, and warning against temptations to which they had once succumbed. This is the language of sinning and saving. But Rorty quickly tempers the fervor of religious zealotry by using the terms "therapeutic" and "edifying." Fire and brimstone preaching gives way to encounter groups. What Rorty presents us with is three mature, calm adults who can counsel us out of our childish struggles with authority figures, who can help us overcome both the manic and the depressive phases of philosophy, and who can counsel us to think for ourselves and to resist the temptations of philosophic and authoritative dogma.

Rorty presents himself and his heroes as our therapists, and he presents the reading of philosophy as a process of therapy. Rorty is a peacemaker rather than a kingmaker.[3] He brings analytic and continental traditions together; he makes everyone into a pragmatist so that we can all sit on a couch and talk together; and he places himself squarely within "we" or "us."[4] Rorty is not alone, and neither is anyone else.

Analytic Rorty, Psychoanalytic Theory, and the Question of the Other

In what follows, I will trace through Rorty's program of therapy as it is illustrated by his oppositional stance toward epistemology.

The "mirror" of *Philosophy and the Mirror of Nature* is traditional philosophy's way of characterizing the relationship between thought and the world.[5] The mind—or later, language—functions as a mirror that reflects more or less accurately what is external to it. Rorty has many disagreements with this image, and with the philosophical problems that arise when philosophers attempt to clarify the mirror image. He also thinks the problems that the mirror was to solve are not really problems at all, or at least are not "interesting" problems.

Rorty's disagreement with the image of mirroring is multifaceted. He does not like the idea that we human beings are essentially knowers; he does not like the idea that the world around us is essentially knowable; and finally, he disagrees with the notion that there is any easy correspondence between knowers and the knowable. The epistemological problematic, then, is wrong on every count.

Looking once again at the bipolar explanation, we can argue that Rorty sees this correspondence between knowers and the knowable as a grandiose and poorly thought-out scheme for organizing things that are not suited to organization. The whole epistemological outlook, which suggests that there is a universal fit between knowers and the knowable, then, is a construct that is doomed to collapse when we come to our senses and realize that we are not mirrors, we are not privileged, and even if we were, there would be nothing to reflect. We need not settle for nihilism, however, because there is *something* for Rorty; it is just not epistemology.

As with many stories of philosophy, Rorty's really gets going with Descartes. Although there is some discussion of ancient and medieval thought, it is in Rorty's discussion of Descartes's dualism and what has historically followed that we can find Rorty's position.

Cartesian dualism answers the skeptic's problem of complete doubt by limiting the realm of doubt to the physical while maintaining a region of certainty in the mental. The doubt that is relegated to the physical is by the end of the Sixth Meditation a highly circumscribed doubt. We know, for Descartes, how our senses work; we have memory; we can tell sleeping from waking. Not only can Descartes notice "all the errors to which [his] nature is liable," but also, he is "able to correct or avoid them" (Descartes, 55).

What the physical/mental distinction does for Descartes in the end is to provide boundaries for the disciplines. Philosophic inquiry tells us that theology does not belong in places where scientists congregate. Philosophy, then, is a border guard who keeps the priests out of the lab.

Cartesian philosophy is manic in that it sees itself as understanding broad swaths of human existence well enough to act as a gatekeeper. Philosophy must comprehend theology and science so that the two are kept separate. Philosophy, then, is the grandiose schemer that underlies all disciplinary distinctions, and is thus responsible for circumscribing inquiry, and hence, for limiting our reading to one floor in the university library, and even to one shelf on that floor.

After discussing Cartesian dualism, Rorty goes on to give a twentieth-century version of what he considers to be still a seventeenth-century problematic. His "Antipodeans" are like human beings in every way except that they perceive all sensation as brain states rather than mental states. These "persons without minds" are the material half of Cartesian dualism, and their experience of "c-fibers" are as uninformative as are human beings' experiences of pains.

The whole Cartesian outlook, then, has been a kind of folly. Instead of its liberating inquiry, it has stifled inquiry; and instead of informing us about the true nature of things, it has told us nothing. We are left with yet another failed mania.

In setting up the collapse of Cartesian dualism, Rorty discusses what he calls "our glassy essence" (Rorty 1979, 42–44).

He writes that within the phrase *"Glassy Essence . . .* are all things which corpses do not have and which are distinctively human" (Rorty 1979, 44). The glassy essence is the mirrorlike part of the mind that reflects the external world and gives us a more or a less accurate picture of the world. It is equally the site of all the mysterious workings of life.

For Rorty, the glassy essence may be an acceptable part of ancient, or of seventeenth-century thought, but it most assuredly should not be a part of our contemporary world. He writes:

> To suggest that there are no universals—that they are *flatus vocis*—is to endanger our uniqueness. To suggest that the mind is the brain is to suggest that we secrete theorems and symphonies as our spleen secretes dark humors. Professional philosophers shy away from these "crude pictures" because they have other pictures—thought to be less crude—which were painted in the later seventeenth century. (Rorty 1979, 43–44)

The only reason we speak of mind/body dualism, for Rorty, is that it sounds less crude to us than would speaking of secretion. The more refined images make us into angelic or godlike beings, spiritual rather than physical. A decided preference for the angelic might well be a kind of manic desire, while settling for secretion might be evidence of depression. Secretion is an ugly term, and depression is characterized by self-loathing.

For Rorty, secretion and spirit are equally useless stories that we tell to explain things that are not worth explaining. No grand schematizing will explain in any interesting way what is going on and neither will nihilism do us any good. For Rorty, then, we should cease to ask "What is going on?" and we should, instead, find a new intellectual pursuit, which he describes in the penultimate chapter of *Philosophy and the Mirror of Nature.*

This new intellectual pursuit is one of two possible roles for philosophers that Rorty identifies. The two roles are first, that of the informed dilettante, the polypragmatic, Socratic intermediary between various discourses. In [this philosopher's] salon, so to speak, hermetic thinkers are charmed out of their self-enclosed practices. Disagreements between disciplines and discourses are compromised or transcended in the course of the conversation. The second role is that of the cultural overseer who knows everyone's common ground—the Platonic philosopher-king who knows what everybody else is really doing whether *they* know it or not, because he knows about the ultimate context (the Forms, the Mind, Language) within which they are doing it. (Rorty 1979, 317–318)

The second role that Rorty discusses, that of a philosopher-king, is the bad role, the one he rejects. It is this role that is manic in its attempts to schematize all human experience. Rorty calls this epistemology and wants to cure us of our epistemic temptations.

Rorty carefully states that he does not want to replace epistemology with a successor, but rather wants to leave a gap where there once was a thing we called epistemology (Rorty 1979, 315). Our new practice, which he terms "hermeneutics" is, for Rorty, a way to break out of the manic/depressive cycle.[6] It is hermeneutic modesty rather than deep melancholia.

The modesty arises from the paradox of the hermeneutic circle, which Rorty characterizes as

the fact that we cannot understand the parts of a strange culture, practice, theory, language, or whatever, unless we know something about how the whole thing works, whereas we cannot get a grasp on how the whole works until we have some understanding of its parts. (Rorty 1979, 319)

Rorty likens this circle to "getting acquainted with a person" (Rorty 1979, 319). When we truly wish to get acquainted with people, we studiously try to avoid prejudice and other totalizing gestures; we open ourselves to others through conversation, and we withhold judgment to the best of our ability. In short, we are nice and we listen. The hermeneutic circle has us getting acquainted within a totalizing framework, but always being suspicious of our judgments and always ready to be proven wrong and consequently always ready to rewrite and rethink.

Hermeneutic modesty, then, provides a seeming middle ground between mania and depression, between grand schematizing and abject nihilism. And it calls for dilettantism rather than for expertise.

The therapeutic situation for Rorty, then, is not Dr. Freud in a large leather chair and Anna O. sprawled on a couch, but rather is a reading and talking room at a library with a bunch of nice, well-read, unpretentious people lounging and getting acquainted with both the exotic and the endogenous.[7]

This process of getting acquainted hermeneutically Rorty terms "edification" (Rorty 1979, 360). He writes:

> The attempt to edify (ourselves or others) may consist in the hermeneutic activity of making connections between our own culture and some exotic culture. . . . But it may instead consist in the "poetic" activity of thinking up new aims, new words, or new disciplines, followed by, so to speak, the inverse of hermeneutics: the attempt to reinterpret our familiar surroundings in the unfamiliar terms of our new inventions. (Rorty 1979, 360)

While there seems to be room for *poesis*, for making and doing, within this account, the Rorty of *Contingency, Irony, and Solidarity* is vastly more interested in reading than he is in writing.[8] He writes:

> So our doubts about our own characters or our own culture can be resolved or assuaged only by enlarging

our acquaintance. The easiest way of doing that is to read books, and so ironists spend more of their time placing books than in placing real live people. (Rorty 1989, 80)

Reading is the consumption of the already existing, and even if all that one reads is synthesized, the product of the synthesis cannot be radically new.[9] Rorty's scheme, then, limits the possibility for change. In the place of the maniacal, creative, underground revolutionary is the calm, liberal, above-board politician who proposes rules changes.

Rorty's need to cure us of our maniacal tendencies without sending us into a deep depression structurally determines his liberal politics. Liberalism carries with it the hope of incremental change over time, and the slow broadening of participation. The hope staves off depression, and the slow pace protects us from mania. Rorty's liberalism, then, is clearly the liberal consumption of the already made, and cannot become the radical making of the new.

Where there is some room for something like writing in Rorty's scheme is where he calls for redescription. He writes:

[The ironist's] method is redescription rather than inference. Ironists specialize in redescribing ranges of objects or events in partially neologistic jargon, in the hope of inciting people to adopt and extend that jargon. An ironist hopes that by the time she has finished using old words in new senses, not to mention brand-new words, people will no longer ask questions phrased in the old words. (Rorty 1989, 78)

First, I note that the ironist incites not rioting but adoption of a "partially neologistic jargon." Second, I note that because the jargon is only partially neologistic, its revolutionary possibility is limited. The new is always spoken in terms of the old and is hence limited by the old. Because the old always exerts conservative force, the possibility of revolution is forestalled.

There are several strands of Rorty's thought that come together to form an antiradicalism both philosophically and politically. To help show Rorty's view, I will quote a long passage. Rorty writes:

> If we adopt this view of new philosophical paradigms nudging old problems aside, rather than providing new ways of stating or solving them, then we will see the second ("impure") type of philosophy of language as a last nostalgic attempt to hook up a new kind of philosophical activity with an old problematic. We will see Dummett's notion of philosophy of language as "first philosophy" as mistaken not because some other area is "first" but because the notion of philosophy as having foundations is as mistaken as that of knowledge having foundations. In this conception, "philosophy" is not a name for a discipline which confronts permanent issues and unfortunately keeps misstating them, or attacking them with clumsy instruments. Rather, it is a cultural genre, a "voice in the conversation of mankind" . . . which centers on one topic rather than another at some given time not by dialectical necessity but as a result of various things happening elsewhere in the conversation (the New Science, the French Revolution, the modern novel) or of individual men of genius who think of something new (Hegel, Marx, Frege, Freud, Wittgenstein, Heidegger), or perhaps the resultant of several such forces. Interesting philosophical change (we might say "philosophical progress," but this would be question-begging) occurs not when a new way is found to deal with an old problem but when a new set of problems emerges and the old ones begin to fade away. The temptation (both in Descartes's

time and in ours) is to think that the new problematic is the old one rightly seen. But, for all the reasons Kuhn and Feyerabend have offered in their criticism of the "textbook" approach to the history of inquiry, this temptation should be resisted. (Rorty 1979, 264)

Within this passage, there is a clear tension between Rorty's tendency for antiradicalism and the possibility of the radically new. Where there is room for the new is in his notion of the "men of genius" who come up with new sets of problems, and in his notion that the history of philosophy is comprised of a series of paradigm shifts rather than of a coherent slow narrative in which we are all trying to do the same thing. Thus, Rorty imports Hegel's world-historical individual, adds in a touch of Foucauldian historical rupture, and thinks he has come up with space for the new.

His antifoundationalism coupled with his statement that philosophy "is a cultural genre . . . which centers on one topic rather than another . . . as a result of various things happening elsewhere in the conversation" work together to contradict radical possibility.

If philosophy is not foundational, not first, then definitionally it must come only in reaction to other things. Philosophy does not lead, it follows. As follower, philosophy cannot be radical, cannot provide space for the new. This notion is bolstered by his statement that philosophy is a result of other cultural phenomena.

Since there are two opposed views, I need to show why one wins out over the other, and thus why Rorty is better thought of as antiradical than as radical. To do this, I will argue that even in his radical moment, there is a major component of antiradicalism, and that there is no radical correlate in his antiradical moment.

The notion that men of genius provide our only chance for major breaks in history is fundamentally antiradical in that it forces us to wait, as if for the messiah, until there is some kind of consensus about this newly emerged thing.

For Kuhn, Einstein is a major break from the Newtonian world, Einstein is new. But Einstein, like all "men of genius," is not socially accepted until he ceases to be new. Because genius requires us to wait, and because we are not capable of recognizing genius, the genius model of historical rupture cannot function as space for radical possibility.

The attempt to identify genius and simultaneously to avoid looking foolish acts as a restraint on radical change. We cannot think of ourselves as geniuses—genius is always other, and we cannot recognize genius because of its status as other. What is genius is what we do not know. The genius model, then, is a check on creativity, on all attempts to break away from the old.[10]

Possible Worlds

and Narrative Convention

I

"Solidarity is not discovered by reflection but created" (Rorty 1989, xvi). That our sense of "we"-ness is so historicized and so aestheticized for Rorty has important consequences for his liberal democratic utopia. Rorty goes on to say that theory is not the genre best able to create feelings of solidarity; rather, this task is best left to "genres such as ethnography, the journalist's report, the comic book, the docudrama, and, especially, the novel" (Rorty 1989, xvi).

The creation of human solidarity is arguably the single most important duty we human beings have, for it is solidarity that will keep us from destroying one another. This project is taken further by ecology, geology, and animal rights activists who argue that it is not human solidarity we need, but rather solidarity with the planet, with the solar system, or at least with sentient beings. The attempts to create this kind of solidarity are found in the stories we tell about "how things, in the broadest possible sense of the term, hang together—in the broadest possible sense of the term" (Rorty 1982, xiv).

Rorty, thus far, has not concerned himself with any narrative creation of solidarity other than that of human solidarity.

Though he could be roundly criticized for this omission, this chapter will focus only on his work on human solidarity, but it is worth noting that his line "The world does not speak. Only we do," has dire consequences for eco-theory (Rorty 1989, 6).

In the passage cited above, Rorty lists several genres that he feels will serve us better than theory in our attempts to make the world less cruel. Since he is so insistent about this point, it is well worth looking closely at these genres, their social milieu, and their positions in Rorty's program.

The first thing to note is that after this sentence, Rorty returns only to novels and ethnographies. Journalism, docudramas, and comic books pretty much drop out of the picture before the pages are given arabic numerals. What is it about these latter three genres that makes them unworthy of discussion? What is it about the other two that makes Rorty come back to them? And finally, what is it about novels that makes Rorty single them out for the modifier "especially"?

Each of these genres is unidirectional. That is, each is produced in one place and consumed in another and the consumers are given no space for reversing the channels of communication, save that of refusing to purchase or consume similar products.

Of the genres Rorty lists, newspapers are the most widely available and offer the closest thing to bidirectionality by offering to print six or seven letters to the editor on any given day. Where newspapers are most limited, perhaps, is in their need to be at least vaguely representational both in reportage and in selection of letters. Newspapers, and all journalism, maintain some tie to the external world.

Docudramas have some of the same limitations as journalism in terms of representationalism, and if the documentary side is being stressed, then film adds to the representational quality. If the drama side is stressed, there are still going to be pictures that might make representationalism at least seem to be a criterion.

Although comic books have pictures, and although recent comic books are dealing with suicide and disease and death, it might be safe to assume that Rorty mentions comic books only to be "nice," but their status vis-à-vis representationalism is probably not what Rorty is concerned about. Comic books are not taken seriously by the cognoscenti and presumably it is this snotty attitude that Rorty, a self-proclaimed snot as a child, is concerned with (Rorty 1993 35).

We are left with novels and ethnographies, two similar, if opposed, narrative conventions. Ethnographies purport to describe the habits, thoughts, and behaviors of exotic people, or of familiar people made exotic through ethnographic conventions. The writing of an ethnography comes after an extended period of observation of a group of "them" by one or more of "us." The ethnographer translates them into us, makes their ways comprehensible to us, and so, in a sense, colonizes them.

Ethnography has a double logic here. First, it requires that there be otherness—a "them" to be the object of study by us subjects. But then, in the course of study, the subject-object polarization must be erased as we come to see that they are like us, that we can understand them and domesticate them. Ethnography, then, needs the exotic even as it needs to destroy the exotic.

The double logic of ethnography is equally that of colonialism in that colonies are also both exotic and endogenous. The colonies are elsewhere, but they are also part of the empire. The difficulties with maintaining this relationship are legion.

The possibility for exploitation in colonialism rests on the tension inherent in the double relation. "They" must be unlike "us" so that the exploitation can be seen as separate from issues of morality, but at the same time, "they" have to be like "us" so that "they" can perform "our" labor.

Ethnography, then, can provide the linguistic support for the practice of colonialism. I would argue further that ethnography is a kind of colonialism. I do not want to conflate ideas and people; rather, I want to argue first that the ideal can occasion the actual, and second, that the ideal makes possible the cultural. That is, ethnography can provide an opening for political colonialism, and it does provide an opening for cultural colonialism. If everyone on the planet is described as a consumer, for example, then the whole planet suddenly becomes open to economic hegemony. This hegemony is precluded under other descriptions of the world. There are, then, real-world effects of vocabularies—some things are made possible and others impossible by discursive practice. This discursive practice is, then, *practice*, and so a vocabulary can be implicated as a colonizer.

The problems with ethnography for Rorty's purposes are twofold. First, ethnography has an unstable status regarding representationalism. Ethnography is not trying to mirror them as they are, but rather is trying to describe them as they appear to us so that our vocabulary can account for them as well. We name their exotic practices as exotic, and by naming them, we make the exotic endogenous. Anything that can be put into our vocabulary ceases to be exotic, and becomes one more thing we have consumed.

This touches on the second point, which is that whatever sense of leftism remains in Rorty's thinking is likely to be uncomfortable with the messy politics of ethnographic colonialism. On the other hand, the creation of human solidarity, of greater and greater we-ness is clearly a kind of colonialism. Rorty's solution for the tension between the desire to ameliorate ethnographic colonialism and the need to make we-ness into a worldwide hegemonic moral imperative is to turn to the world of novels.

Novels are both free from the demands of representationalism, and bound by what takes the place of representationalism for Rorty—the familiar. That is, novels are not required to be glassy essences that show reality as it is, for there is no such thing as reality as it is. What novels need to do, however, is to move us smoothly from one vocabulary to another, from a redescription to a re-redescription.

In order to move us across vocabularies, novels must start with what is most familiar, what makes us feel for a time that we are inside the novel.[1] Through measured steps, a novel can take us to less familiar terrain, but only by putting the new in the vocabulary of the familiar, only by inviting in, tempting us to turn pages, seducing us with a heady mixture of the exotic and the known.

The metaphor here is deliberately mixed and deliberately sexual because when Rorty liberates us from the necessity of representation and makes solidarity a creation, he is left with desire and aesthetics as positive motivators, and fear as a negative motivator.

When our ethical sensibility becomes a made thing rather than a found thing, the result is not so much that "anything goes" as it is that the creation of ethics, the aesthetic of duty becomes the foremost concern of society. Rorty's emphasis on privacy and his discussion of the shame he felt over his private, if sublimated, sexual desire is part and parcel of the aestheticization of the ethical. (See Chapter 3 for biographical details.)

The novel as a genre is in the position of the seductress inviting the unsuspecting virgin in, making the potential conquest feel safe but on edge. There is something different, but all the words still seem so familiar that the difference is as yet inexplicable. Wary but titillated, the reader turns yet another page, goes deeper into the novel's lair, further into a new vocabulary. This new vocabulary, as seductress, must maintain a careful balance between titillation and terror, between the new and the familiar. Anything too radical will scare off readers or potential conquests.

What novels must do then, in striking this balance, is to be real accounts of fictional people. That is, novels are bound by convention, by the desire to be read and consumed, to stay within familiar terrain. Once bound by conventions of familiarity, novels come very close to representationalism. Thus familiarity takes the place of the real. If it is not the "real" world that novels represent, but only the "familiar" world, we should wonder if this difference is at all substantial, or if Rorty is slipping back into the history of epistemology and the vocabulary of representationalism and some version of realism.

It would be helpful to contrast, once again, the genre of novels with that of ethnographies. If novels are real accounts of fictional people, then perhaps ethnographies are fictional accounts of real people. That is, ethnographies are created vocabularies recognized as such, but are based on actually existing people and practices. This distinction is akin to Rorty's distinction between Nietzsche and Proust. Rorty writes:

> As a first crude way of blocking out a difference between Proust and Nietzsche we can note that Proust became who he was by reacting against and redescribing people—real live people whom he had met in the flesh—whereas Nietzsche reacted against and redescribed people he had met in books. Both men wanted to create themselves by writing a narrative about the people who had offered descriptions of them. . . .
>
> The difference between people and ideas is, however, only superficial. (Rorty 1989, 100)

In the light of this passage, we could say that Proust is doing ethnography and Nietzsche is writing novels. This passage shows that ethnographies and novels collapse into one genre that we might call "strong redescription." What makes possible this collapse of genre types is first that each maintains a moment of familiarity-cum-representationalism, and second that, for Rorty, there is only a "superficial" difference between people and ideas. The deep level (e.g., "reality") and the surface level (e.g., "ideology") are brought together in the collapse of ethnography and fiction, in the translation of representationalism into the vocabulary of familiarity.

Proust's *Remembrance of Things Past* becomes, for Rorty, a fictional ethnography and Nietzsche's works become ethnographic fiction. As long as Rorty allows us to equate people and ideas, the basis for a narrative drops out—that is, it no longer matters if the people are real or not. All that is left is the set of conventions that govern narrative structure.

Before I look at the political consequences of this version of narrativity, I would like to look again at Rorty's discussion of the Antipodeans in *Philosophy and the Mirror of Nature* with an eye toward tracing a genealogy of narrative thinking in Rorty's work.

Rorty's discussion of the Antipodeans is one in a long series of discussions of possible worlds in analytic philosophy. The general conventions of possible-world-talk are that we are asked to imagine a place in which things are different from the place we are in right now. Our failure or success in this kind of imagining is meant to show something about necessity and possibility, or about the rules of logic. It is no stretch at all to see that possible-world-talk is a subgenre of novels.

Rorty introduces the Antipodeans to us as a way of showing that neither the physical reductionism of c-fiber stimulation, nor the mentalistic talk of pain perception gives us anything interesting, worthwhile, or even different. A possible world of physicalism and brain states turns out to look very much like the "real" world of mentalism and mind-states. In either world, pain is pain and we know of one another's pain through pain behavior.[2] In this way, fiction can be edifying, can shed light on the "real" world, and can help us redescribe ourselves. Specifically, the Antipodean story is meant to make us stop talking about both mentalism and physicalism.

The more interesting points are first the way that Rorty gets us to see his point, and second, the fact that he uses fictional pain as an edifying tool. The Antipodeans function as the exotic that is still familiar, the strangers who are like us in every respect except one seemingly crucial one that turns out not to be so crucial. As the discussion moves along, the "they" turns out to be pretty much like the "we," and so Rorty can generously expand his notion of "we" without really compromising the we-ness of us.

To go back to the notions of seduction, familiarity and the new, the Antipodeans are like us and so are familiar, and we can comfortably enter into the "novel." Then we discover a crucial difference, but we are comforted by the basic familiarity of the situation. Finally, all the tension is relieved because they are we after all. What seemed new and daring for a titillating moment turns out to be the familiar all along. And since vocabulary shifts are, for Rorty, gradual and generally not noticed, we are never on unfamiliar ground. The safety of the "we" is always a safe haven, a place to retreat to when there is too much unfamiliarity.

The second point I want to touch on is Rorty's use of pain. In the end, what makes every assimilation possible for Rorty is either the presence of pain or the possibility of pain. What separates the Antipodeans from us Terrestrials is that we *talk* differently about pain. What unites us all is that we all can feel pain.

Rorty's story of historical progress is a story in which we become more linguistically open to other people's pain.[3] The more alike we find one another to be in terms of vulnerability to pain, the nicer we are to one another. The pain Rorty singles out is humiliation—a specifically human pain that arises out of the linguistic ability of human beings.[4] We are all susceptible to being redescribed in ways that make our self-descriptions look pathetic; and since all there is to a person is a self-description (the result of a brand of anti-essentialism), a person can, in effect, be negated at the drop of a name.

By keying on humiliation and the hurling of redescriptions, Rorty misses out on a lot of issues that need to be discussed. Much interesting work has recently been done on issues about bodies, about embodied pain and embodied subjectivity, but Rorty seems more concerned about the psychic aftermath of torture than about the real physical pain of torture.

When Rorty's liberal utopia is one of people reading, redescribing, and reacting to redescriptions, we have to wonder just what has happened to bodies and to embodied pain. As Rebecca Comay writes:

> His *exclusion* of philosophy from the political sphere
> is paralleled precisely by his *idealization* of politics, his

onesided emphasis on discursive practices (to the neglect of, e.g., work and power), his overvaluation of the cultural sphere. (Comay, 123)

When Rorty writes that there is little difference between people and ideas, he is doing precisely what Comay charges him with, namely, idealizing the interactions of people in the political sphere and ignoring the embodied nature of pain and of people. Pain is not simply an idea, a response to a negative review of a journal article; rather, it can be a real body's signal that something physical is terribly wrong, and that some physical response is necessary.

A consequence of Rortian idealization is the legitimation of fictions and of possible world talk as effective argumentative and edifying strategies. That is, if everything is to be treated at the level of ideas and not at the level of bodies, then it becomes perfectly acceptable to spend one's days reading at home rather than spending one's days at soup kitchens. Admittedly, in Rorty's liberal utopia, there will not be soup kitchens, but it is not even slightly reasonable to think that there will not be physical pain.[5] We cannot be a world of private readers and university professors as long as we are people with bodies.

What goes along with this notion of people as private readers and self-creators whose bodies have dropped out of the picture is a kind of *National Geographic* voyeurism. That is, we venture into the exotic world of bodies and bodies-in-pain and bodies breast-feeding long enough to be titillated and shocked and amused, and then we return safely to our disembodied being-as-reader.

If Rorty gives us the largest possible "we" that no longer has room for the exotic, this still is not a guarantee against humiliation. Liberal high-minded people are often the ones who say things like "I'm Jewish so it's okay for me to tell an anti-Semitic joke," or "I'm Black, so I can use the word 'nigger.' " Being one of us, feeling community, saying "we" is perhaps not really a useful way of thinking or speaking.

Rorty's world is one in which people do not go out into the world, as it were; Rorty's strong poet does not live *with* people, and it seems that the liberal tendencies we are to have do not necessarily make *with* into the most common prepositional attitude. The only sense of "with-ness" we get in Rorty comes from our reading the same books and feeling some of the same fears. This is a very limited sense of community, a very restricted sense of community, and in the end is not very communal.[6] In the next chapter, I will offer a reading of Rorty's notion of community by drawing from his autobiographical essay, "Trotsky and the Wild Orchids." Before I do this, however, I would like to look further at the aestheticization issue and its relationship to Rorty's notion of cruelty.

II

Rorty is clearly aware of the cruel side of redescription. Not only does he explicitly state that "redescription often humiliates," he also sets up the public/private distinction in part to protect the public from the ironist (Rorty 1989, 90). Rorty gives us, then, two kinds of cruelty—the idealized aesthetic kind that arises from redescription, and the political kind that arises from oppression. But as Rebecca Comay notes, Rorty's emphasis is on idealized and aestheticized cruelty.

The public/private split renders aesthetic cruelty *merely* aesthetic and ensures the complete depoliticization of the aesthetic. If every creation is simultaneously a destruction, then creation is inherently cruel, but if creation is always *merely* aesthetic and never political, then this aesthetic cruelty is a victimless crime, a purely self-regarding act, and so is allowed by John Stuart Mill's liberalism, which Rorty says "is pretty much the last word" (Rorty 1989, 63).

At this point, I want to turn to Jacques Derrida's reading of Antonin Artaud in Derrida's essay "The Theater of Cruelty." What this essay gives us is an understanding of the nature of aesthetic cruelty, the desire to be originary, and the impossibility of fully realizing this desire. That Rorty is concerned with these issues we can see in the following passage:

> We shall see the conscious need of the strong poet to *demonstrate* that he is not a copy or replica as merely a special form of the unconscious need everyone has: the need to come to terms with the blind impress which chance has given him, to make a self for himself by redescribing that impress in terms which are, if only marginally, his own. (Rorty 1989, 43)

This coming to terms with the blind impress (a reference to a Philip Larkin poem that Rorty discusses), is Rorty's way of saying that we all want to speak for ourselves by redescribing everyone else as accidental players in our own histories of necessity. As Fraser has noted, Rorty has a strong Romantic streak in him that makes him see humans as all desiring to be the individual heroes of their own lives. This purportedly universal desire is unfortunately asocial, and even more unfortunately based on a metaphor of language and self-description as private property, but more on this later.

In Derrida's reading, Artaud's theater of cruelty is a theater without an author, without authority and its trappings, and without a script that has been written according to the rules of written language. The cruelty of this theater appears on four levels. First, there is the cruelty of the foundation sacrifice—the killing of the father (God/the author); second, there is the cruelty of freedom—turning the orphaned, de-scripted people loose into a space that is no longer a stage, and stranding them with none of the props to which actors are accustomed; third, there is the cruelty of stripping from the orphans any secretly harbored hope of finding an original truth to represent; and fourth, there is the necessity that a life force carries with it, the necessity of committing parricide and consequently being orphaned, the necessity of destroying in order to create, the necessity of living and dying. There is here, an eternal return of murder and abandonment.

The theater of cruelty signifies the destruction of all classical forms of representation, the destruction of mimesis, "the most naive form of representation" (Derrida 1987, 234). Derrida writes, "Theatrical art should be the primordial and privileged site of this destruction of imitation; more than any other art, it has been marked by the labor of total representation in which the affirmation of life lets itself be doubled and emptied by negation" (Derrida 1987, 234).

It is within the theater, where representation is all, that we can see the clearest version of the kind of representation that underlies all of Western "religious, philosophies, and politics" (Derrida 1987, 224). In the traditional theater, all is predetermined by a script that has been predetermined by an author's relation to the structures of language, life, and the presentation of life within language.

The written script for a play can be seen as a metaphor for the script of all of God's Creation, and the author of a play is, equally, the Author of Creation. What there is then, is an original version with original intentions and we the actors are all playing out that original version, are all reading that script, with more or less acting ability.

Within the logic of the play, or within the economy of representationalism, actors, people, are interchangeable. Individuals lose their significance except insofar as they are signs for some other meaning. That is, individuals, within an economy of representation, are fungible, they are the coinage to be exchanged for things of greater import. Within the theater, the thing of greater import is the presentation of an author's creation according to the author's will. Within Creation, the thing of greater import is the divined Divine Will.

As Derrida writes, the theater of cruelty would signal the end of "the sensory illustration of a text already written . . . the repetition of a *present* . . . a presentation of the present (Derrida 1987, 237). What would now come into play is "representation . . . as the autopresentation of pure visibility and even pure sensibility" (Derrida 1987, 238).

The new theater would be, then, one without mediation between life and living. There would be no language which represents thought to the world or the world to thought. Derrida writes that speech and writing "will once more become *gestures*" in that the body, which is "purloin[ed]" by the "*logical*," by the logos, will return to its rightful place in articulation (Derrida 1987, 240). The dominance of the logos over communication, the reliance on the word without regard to its being written or spoken, leaves the body in the position of the actor, of the mime. One aspect of the logic of language requires signifiers to disappear into the signified, and the body, as carrier of the signifier must equally disappear. This logic holds for a representational notion of language because what is important within language as representation is the thing being represented, the thing that is the truth.

A representational notion of language, then, violently "disappears" the body so that it may carry out its task of revealing the truth. The theater of cruelty ends this violence and replaces it with its own kind of cruelty. It should be stressed that the theater of cruelty is not an introduction of cruelty into human life, but rather is a substitution of one kind of cruelty for another.

Representational notions of language require mediation between what is real and what is expressed. This process of mediation is a kind of violence done to all parties in the relation. To the extent to which the mediator is inadequate for its task, the truth suffers; to the extent to which the mediator must disappear, the mediator suffers; and to the extent to which we need truth to emerge from the economy of representation, we suffer.

Essentialism falls under this representational rubric, and it also must be left behind. Essentialism's cruelties include the amputation of the accidental, the suffocation of creative thought and creative action, and the dismemberment of the body as the by-product of the hegemony of the spiritual.

What remains after the theater of cruelty has destroyed so much of the occidental tradition? To borrow an image from this tradition, perhaps there is something akin to the Kantian manifold without the possibility of Kantian space and time, and without the possibility of the categories of the understanding. Derrida writes:

> Glossopoeia, which is neither an imitative language nor a creation of names, takes us back to the borderline of the moment when the word has not yet been born, when articulation is no longer a shout but not yet discourse, when repetition is *almost* impossible, and along with it, language in general. . . . This is the eve of the origin of languages, and of the dialogue between theology and humanism whose unextinguishable reoccurrence has never not been maintained by the metaphysics of Western theater. (Derrida 1987, 240)

There is, within the theater of cruelty, an overriding desire for the end of dichotomous thought and for the creation of a kind of unity of being. Instead of "the separation of concept and sound, of signified and signifier, of the pneumatical and the grammatical, the freedom of translation and tradition, the movement of interpretation, the difference between the soul and the body, the master and the slave, God and man, author and actor," instead of these oppositions, which are and have always been sources of cruelty, there would be, perhaps, unschematized experience. (Derrida could easily have added to this list "man and woman," "parent and child," "cruelty and kindness.")

What we have is a kind of permanent revolution without repetition, permanent flux. And yet, Derrida writes that for Artaud, "it is known that the representations of the theater of cruelty had to be painstakingly determined in advance. The absence of an author and his text does not abandon the stage to dereliction. . . . Everything, thus, will be *prescribed* in a writing and a text whose fabric will no longer resemble the model of classical representation" (Derrida 1987, 239).

The question still remains what is this new (old?) kind of representation, this autopresentation that is always originary, and yet "painstakingly determined in advance." Within this "prescribed" text is the space of self-creation at every moment. Living is the playing out of the prescribed and still originary script. In the banal sense, it is the playing out of a new and original, but still recognizable, life. That is, each person in the play is unique and original, but is recognizably human and plays out an obviously human script. In this way, one can be both self-creative and representative of others.

The more radical sense of autopresentation suggests giving up entirely all that is recognizably human and replacing it with what is genuinely self-creative and defiant of categorization. Derrida writes that "the idea of a theater without representation [is] the idea of the impossible" (Derrida 1987, 249).

What do we gain from thinking of the impossible, from condemning representation and ennobling cruelty?[7] We can come to understand what pure creation is. Just as we are cruel in committing parricide so that we may ourselves become creators, so any creator we divined previously must have been equally cruel. There is a fundamental—a foundational—cruelty of creation. This cruelty denies all that has come before and insists on a new order in its own terms. Every act of pure creation is a destruction of all that is previous. This destruction is radical, is a destruction of even the roots of the previous. Pure creation is pure cruelty.

"Cruelty" here, is not to be taken as physical torture. Artaud writes:

> This Cruelty is a matter of neither sadism nor bloodshed, at least not in any exclusive way.
> I do not systematically cultivate horror. The word "cruelty" must be taken in a broad sense, and not in the rapacious physical sense that it is customarily given. (Artaud, 101)

Elsewhere, Artaud writes:

> I employ the word "cruelty" in the sense of an appe-
> tite for life, a cosmic rigor and implacable necessity,
> in the gnostic sense of a living whirlwind that de-
> vours the Darkness, in the sense of that pain apart
> from whose ineluctable necessity life could not
> continue. . . . When the hidden god creates, he obeys
> the cruel necessity of creation. (Artaud, 102)

Artaud's embrace of cruelty is as vigorous as Rorty's embrace is
tenuous. Rorty has a clear sense that the kind of originary self-
creation that Artaud cherishes is indeed cruel, but because Rorty
holds on dearly to his liberalism, he has no choice but to limit the
cruelty to the private sphere.

What we see here is a constant tension in Rorty's work
between his Romantic tendencies and his liberal and pragmatic
tendencies.[8] It is this tension that Nancy Fraser identifies in her
essay "Solidarity or Singularity? Richard Rorty between Romanticism and Technocracy." Fraser suggests that Rorty has had
three ways of dealing with this tension over time. The first two
are the "invisible hand" conception and the "sublimity or decency?" conception (Fraser, 94). The first suggests that the Romantic and the pragmatic support one another; and the second
suggests that they are antithetical and that one must choose
one or the other. The third conception is "partition" (Fraser, 95).
Partition separates the public from the private with, in Rorty's
words, "a firm distinction."

On the consequences of this distinction, Fraser writes:

> As a result, radical theorizing assumes individualistic
> connotations, becoming the very antithesis of collec-
> tive action and political practice. Radical theory, in
> other words, gets inflected as a sphere apart from
> collective life, a sphere of privacy and of individual
> self-fashioning. . . .
>
> The privatization of radical theory takes its toll,
> too, on the shape of the political. In Rorty's hands,

politics assumes an overly communitarian and sol-
idary character, as if in reaction against the extreme
egotism and individualism of his conception of
theory. . . . Here Rorty homogenizes social space, assuming tendentiously that there are no deep social
cleavages capable of generating conflicting solidarities
and opposing "we's." (Fraser, 103–104)

Fraser argues then that because Rorty's conception of the radical
is so individualistic and parricidal, he really has no choice but
to privatize it; and because his conception of the political is so
communitarian, he has no choice but to limit its space so that
people will have some sense of a nonhegemonized self.

Artaud would allow an author to give scripts to actors, and
would allow the actors to speak the humiliating words of a
script; Rorty, on the other hand, finds that the cruelty of Artaud's
theater is impermissible. Artaud makes cruelty public through
the notions of theater and of speech; Rorty makes cruelty private through the notions of reading and redescribing for private
purposes.

Not only does Rorty's conception of the radical force him
into antiradicalism, so also does his conception of vocabulary
shifts. There are two key strands in Rorty's conception of vocabulary shifts that lock him into antiradicalism, and these are the
genius theory and the family resemblance theory. Each is em-
blematic of one side of the romantic/pragmatic split.

The genius theory of vocabulary shifts (which is discussed
at the end of chapter one) has us waiting around for a strong
poet to tell us what to think and how to speak. But, of course,
genius is precisely that which goes unrecognized until it is too
late, until everyone has caught on, until the messiah is dead.

Genius is always belated because change only occurs when
it is so overdetermined that "change" is not really the right
word for the imperceptible difference between what came before and the present age. The Romantic embrace of genius, then,
does not serve anyone but the geniuses themselves, who are free

to try to be geniuses in Rorty's account. Because no one will recognize genius until it is long gone, there comes to be a cultural attitude of waiting.

For Rorty, waiting is taken up with reading. We read to find genius that will change not only how we speak, but will further change the topics on which we speak. Because these changes will come only through our recognizing what we read, we will never really see genius as genius.

The result of the genius theory of vocabulary shifts is, paradoxically, that there is no genius theory of vocabulary shifts. The Romantic Man of Genius goes unrecognized until it is too late.[9]

On the pragmatic side is Wittgensteinian family resemblance. Wittgenstein writes that

> We see a complicated network of similarities overlapping and criss-crossing; sometimes overall similarities, sometimes similarities of detail. . . . I can think of no better expression to characterize these similarities than "family resemblances"; for the various resemblances between members of a family: build, features, colour of eyes, gait, temperament, etc. etc. overlap and criss-cross in the same way. —And I shall say: "games" for a family. (Wittgenstein, sections 66–67)

The criterion for inclusion in a family, in this view, is some kind of likeness. While Wittgenstein refuses to give a theory of likeness along the lines of essentialism or natural kinds, he still privileges likeness as a classificatory scheme.

Because our ability to understand or know anything is predicated on our having a socially determined context in which to put the matter at hand, we become locked into our social positions. An anti-essentialism that has no mechanism for allowing us to deal with the unfamiliar, with the alien or the unrelated, is as susceptible to cruelty as are the essentialisms that Rorty wants to get out of.

Rorty's pragmatic response to the earnest and impatient desire for change is to put on the airs of historical perspective and the wisdom of the ages. With this tone, Rorty writes:

> Henry Gates, Deborah McDowell, and other specialists in Afro-American literature have helped rescue from oblivion Zora Neale Hurston's novel *Their Eyes Were Watching God*. People who got Ph.D. degrees in English during the 1980s are as likely to have read this novel as those who got their Ph.D.'s in the 1950s were to have read *The Diary of Anne Frank*, or as those who got their Ph.D.'s in the 1920s were to have read *The Mill on the Floss*. My fifteen-year-old daughter is currently being assigned *The Diary of Anne Frank*. I think it quite likely that my granddaughter I may have will, while in high school, be assigned *Their Eyes Were Watching God*. If she is, she will be a lot better informed about American history, rural poverty, and being black than I was at her age, and will be a more useful citizen in consequence. (Rorty 1991a, 138)

Temporally, Rorty speaks for most of the twentieth century in this passage and for three generations of people. There is a real sense of slow progress—from star-crossed lovers to the Holocaust and then to slavery—our historical ability to empathize widens as we read. "Progress," here, assumes that we not forget past lessons, however. In the next paragraph of this essay, Rorty details how hearing a paper by Eve Kosovsky Sedgwick made him realize that gay high school students really ought to be able to talk to gay high-school counselors, and that denying this is a form of child abuse. When he was in high school, Rorty notes, he thought that antisodomy laws were "commonsensical" (Rorty 1991a, 138).

What is disturbing about this brand of anti-essentialism is that Rorty seems to be a prisoner of his social situation, and even of his current reading.[10] Family resemblance theory limits our vision and thought to what is familiar, to what fits in to our current vocabulary. And it is only environmental and experiential exposure to another, but still related, vocabulary that allows us to change.

Change, under family resemblance theory, must be overdetermined and belated because the change occurs only when the orphan, as it were, turns out to be a long-lost brother or cousin. Without the resemblance, there is no recognition and hence no inclusion.

Overdetermination breeds both political passivity and an inability to think for oneself. Rorty was a less-good citizen as a child than will be his granddaughter because no one told him about rural poverty and blacks. He could not think for himself because his account makes such thought impossible. So Rorty waits to find a new book about a new kind of pain, and when that book crosses his path, he discovers a new kind of pain. These discoveries are reactive, not proactive. And they require a generational passivity in the same way that trickle-down economics requires class passivity.

This passivity is, I would argue, much less a product of the wisdom of the historian's perspective, and much more a result of Rorty's—and Wittgenstein's—privileging of the familiar. This privileging, when coupled with Rorty's liberal toleration of the unfamiliar, is meant to set an acceptable political course for the ship of state. The familiar is what defines the state as a cohesive "we" who can act in concert, and toleration is supposed to enable there to be justice for the "not-we."

Those who are tolerated are not, however, included. They are stigmatized—if only by the label "not-we"—and as stigmatized, they are excluded. The excluded ones are asked to wait. They wait for an engaging and talented novelist to tell their story. Then they wait for Henry Louis Gates, Jr., or his alter ego. Then they wait for college students to read the novel. Then they wait for high school counselors to read the novel. Then they wait for curriculum boards, school district budgets, parents, and teachers. Then they wait for universal literacy. After all of this waiting, they—or their great-grandchildren—are finally heard and their pain is recognized. Then they wait for laws to be passed.

It would seem that Rorty embodies the historian's patience—a patience born of distance, privilege, and relative comfort. It would seem, further, than if anyone is "turning essentialist at the last minute" it is Rorty, who, after all, essentializes reading and waiting and the public/private distinction, to say the least (Rorty 1991a, 136).

If Artaud's notion of the originary is to serve any purpose at all, it might be that it gives us one way to think around or out of our current situation. What is unfortunate about Artaud's theater of cruelty, and Rorty's/Bloom's strong poet is that both conceive of the originary as parricidal. Artaud embraces parricide, while Rorty privatizes it so that no one really gets hurt.

Is there, then, a way to preserve narrative without falling into the traps Rorty does? Without the aestheticization of cruelty, the emphasis on the familiar, the titillation of the exotic, the overromanticization of the parricidal theater of cruelty?

Here I would argue that there is, and the basic move is away from reading the accounts of others to creating one's own accounts. But this creation is not that of the lone romantic writer standing against all of history. Rather, the move lies in deprivatizing, in telling stories directly to other people so that there is an immediate audience who can participate and listen by turns.

There is a wonderful account of the kind of story telling I find to be a good alternative in Vivian Gussin Paley's book *The Boy who Would Be a Helicopter*. The book presents the story of a year in Paley's preschool class, and details in particular the way a boy named Jason slowly finds peace and comfort in a group of children. At the beginning of the year, Jason plays alone in a corner with an imaginary helicopter that makes loud noises and often needs to be fixed. Whenever Jason gets stressed, his helicopter suddenly breaks and he runs away to fix it.

While Jason is working on rotating blades, other children are working out anxieties by being lost children, mommies and babies, superheroes, and fairy-tale characters. The children dictate stories to Paley (usually two or three lines) and then they pick people to act out their stories. There is a general fluidity in the telling of stories and often children change parts to suit the actors.

Very slowly over the course of the year, Jason's disruptive helicopter begins to be integrated into other stories and finally, so does Jason. In the end, he is much more fluid and accepting of a variety of roles than he was in the beginning.

Of course, Paley's story-telling techniques are presented as part of preschool and so the first question might be just how relevant is this for adults. My response is that being a teacher or a mother or a doctor is not so far from being a helicopter or a lost child in the woods. Social roles are precisely that—roles we adopt, though with greater tenacity perhaps than even Jason does with his helicopter.

A social ideal I see lurking in Paley's classroom is the kind of honesty and fluidity the children manage in telling their own stories and participating in the stories of others. The children are often, though not always, willing to adapt their work for the sake of others. Not only would such adaptability make for greater social peace, it would also, I would argue, make for healthier psyches.

All forms of social prejudice can be seen as a kind of story telling, but one that is rigid and so is closed to changes in perception. Being more open not only to one's own perception but even more to the story telling of others is a good way to get past a variety of assumptions about others that form the foundation for injustice. When multiculturalism is seen as story telling and story playing the result is a move away from the reification of genetic and cultural categories and toward the more helpful idea that these categories are social roles we can step in and out of.

Social space must be made, then, for people to step—both in and out of roles. Just as the children in Paley's classroom let Jason be a helicopter and then stop being a helicopter, so must people be allowed these choices without the assumptions that generally accompany social roles.

Just as Marx had us farming in the morning and fishing in the afternoon, so I would have us let loose of individual identities not merely during various parts of the day, but throughout the day. The ideal types that stand behind titles like "mother" or "doctor" or "professional" or "coal miner" or "waitress" or "welfare mother" do nothing but set us up for failure. Plato argues that when one fails to live up to one's function, one is not being what one is. That is, a doctor is not a doctor when the patient dies and a shipbuilder is not a shipbuilder when the boat sinks. Identities hold only with success, and failure strips us of our meaning.

Even if we do not hold so tightly to Platonic notions, still we manage to convince ourselves that we are betraying something if we are less than perfect. Bad mothers, traitors to their kind, being unprofessional—these all connote failure to live up to what is actually an impossible ideal. If, however, we move away from the ideal as identity and move instead toward the notion of role playing, then we will find ourselves less harshly judged for our inevitable failures to live up to the ideal. No doctor has never lost a patient, no mother has never been distracted from perfect attention to her child, and no engineer has never made a design mistake. The mistakes come, rather, from our notion of the ideal.

What I think we ground our notion of the ideal on is a firm distinction between the child and the adult. The child lacks identity, the child plays, the child is innocent and ignorant and preresponsible. The adult has a fixed identity, the adult works, the adult knows and takes responsibility. It is clear, however, from Paley's work that children do things we usually consider grown-up, and it is equally clear from my experience that adults do things we would consider childlike. Given that these categories are not so hard and fast, it seems worthwhile to consider how adding elements associated with children to adult life might actually enrich that life.

Rorty's notion of narrative seems to be limited to the private writing of novels and the private reading of novels. There is no contact between writer and reader save through published articles and books. In Paley's classroom, by contrast, author, actor, and audience are able together during the creation and the playing out and watching of the story. Because the story making is public, it is a fluid process and is expressive not merely of private experience, but also of group experience. Story making done in groups, then, is qualitatively different from that done privately. It is grounded on a different notion of identity and responsibility, and it has a different censor with different limits.

Private creation responds only to its own needs, expresses only its own concerns and is limited only by its own psychic make-up. It refuses to take account of others and assumes, instead, that the individual is isolated and paramount. The hyperindividualism that underlies Rorty's account of creation leads to the constant anxiety that I, the creator, am not merely unique, I am also weird. (The notion of the isolated creator is taken up more fully in Chapter 4.)

In the theater of Paley, we find children creating stories that express private experiences and anxieties like the birth of a new sibling or parental and familial tensions, as well as group experiences like the story someone else just told. By speaking their anxieties and adding elements of common experience, the children manage to get away from feelings of isolation. They connect inner psychic experiences and their home life to their school life. The result is both a wholeness of being without disconnection and a fluidity that allows the children to go from their own stories to those of other children. The result is a sense of the connection each child's own story has to the stories of others.

There still remains the question of the child who refuses to join. Paley's book is cast as a drama that focuses on whether or not Jason and his helicopter will join in and be accepted. First comes acceptance by the group, and in the end comes a careful but willing membership on Jason's part. But one can imagine a child who refuses to join for perfectly legitimate reasons. Here, Rorty's account has an important value in that he maintains that the private is legitimate and is a crucial counterweight to the public. (This issue will be taken up in chapter 5.)

What I would argue first is that Rorty's private realm is all-encompassing and leaves no space for nonprivate connection to others, and second that public space needs to be cast in a fundamentally welcoming fashion. So far, our culture has seemingly come up with only two ways to handle private shame, Rorty's reading of novels under the blanket late at night (a frequent theme in coming out of the closet stories as well as in sad childhood stories) and watching daytime talk shows in which the object of shame is transformed into the object of titillation. Neither of these methods is particularly humane or welcoming. Both demand a long history of isolation, shame, and suffering before connection is made, and the connection is between a person and a book or an image on television rather than between two people who can become friends.

A public commitment to the fostering of noncommercial space for meeting others might include greater Internet access without the market's interference and more events, parades, concerts, and lectures that present a variety of nonmainstream views (more like the controversial NEA awards than like a 4-H fair). Just as Paley's kids are given a variety of stories to bounce off of and daily opportunities to tell and act out their own stories, so the public ought to provide these opportunities to itself. The problem, though, with this notion of broadening is that there is little tolerance of "helicopters," and little tolerance of behavior that is not regulated by the market.

This is where my notion of friendship comes in. An act of friendship in this case would be the acceptance of something unfamiliar in the world, for example, sex on the Internet. One does not have to go to a person whose sex life one finds distressing and offer to have sex with that person in order to be a friend. Rather, at the minimum, one must allow space for story telling. A more welcoming act of friendship might include the telling of inclusive stories.

Using Paley's classroom as a model, we can see that at first the children just let Jason play with his helicopter and fix the blades whenever they broke. Gradually, the children began telling stories with helicopters in them, and finally, sometimes Jason was comfortable enough to let go of the helicopter and be something else for a while.

What I would advocate as a public goal, then, is making space for Jason and his helicopter. In the process, we will reach Rorty's goal of increased solidarity and decreased cruelty, but without the isolation, alienation, and shame that seem to be at the heart of Rorty's retreat from the public sphere.

CHAPTER THREE

Negative Solidarity

While *Philosophy and the Mirror of Nature* is largely a negative work in that it is mostly concerned with ending philosophy, with debunking the metaphysical and epistemic outlooks, it does present a positive program of sorts. This chapter will examine Rorty's positive program in the light of his autobiographical essay "Trotsky and the Wild Orchids."

In *Philosophy and the Mirror of Nature*, Rorty writes of his program:

> Since "education" sounds a bit too flat, and *Bildung* a bit too foreign, I shall use "edification" to stand for the project of finding new, better, more interesting, more fruitful ways of speaking. The attempt to edify (ourselves or others) may consist in the hermeneutic activity of making connections between our own culture and some exotic culture or historical period, or between our own discipline and another discipline which seems to pursue incommensurable aims in an incommensurable vocabulary. But it may instead consist in the "poetic" activity of thinking up such new aims, new words, or new disciplines, followed by, so

to speak, the inverse of hermeneutics: the attempt to reinterpret our familiar surroundings in the unfamiliar terms of our new inventions. (Rorty 1979, 360)

What Rorty's program of edification requires is first a series of oppositions between the exotic and the endogenous, between us and them or now and earlier, and second a real belief that such differences can be squared in a new and improved vocabulary. There is a contradiction of sorts between these two requirements.

If there is real, meaningful opposition between two groups of people or two disciplines, then finding some new vocabulary that ends the opposition is either not possible, or consists in doing violence to one or both of the parties. If the new vocabulary is easily created, then the original opposition was illusory.[1]

The way that Rorty works through this dilemma is first to privatize both meaningful opposition and the violence inherent in dealing with such opposition, and second, to make the public sense of solidarity so general as to be basically meaningless. In *Contingency, Irony and Solidarity*, Rorty writes that the liberal ironist

> thinks that what unites her with the rest of the species is not a common language but *just* susceptibility to pain and in particular to that special sort of pain which the brutes do not share with the humans—humiliation. On her conception, human solidarity is not a matter of sharing a common truth or a common goal but of sharing a common selfish hope, the hope that one's world—the little things around which one has woven into one's final vocabulary—will not be destroyed. (Rorty 1989, 92)

Solidarity, for Rorty, is based solely on each person's desire not to have his or her idiosyncrasies judged in the court of reason. What we share, then, is precisely that which we do not share; that is, we all have idiosyncrasies that by definition are individualized and so not shared. Our idiosyncracity (for lack of a better word) is generalized further to "susceptibility to . . . humiliation." Rorty thinks that saying that people are the beings who can be humiliated is saying enough, and indeed, that saying any more would be tantamount to reentering the metaphysico-epistemological fray. Rorty cannot give us a " 'reason' not to be cruel to those whose final vocabularies are very unlike ours" because offering such a reason would require a metaphysical theory (Rorty 1989, 88). Rorty wants us to get beyond needing reasons for not inflicting pain.

What is to replace reasons, for Rorty, is a feeling—a feeling of solidarity with other people, which feeling is based on one's own sense of alienated idiosyncrasy. We must be sufficiently isolated from one another and sufficiently privatized that we do not start thinking in metaphysical terms. That is, we cannot form a meaningful, positive, public we because it is this kind of we that starts thinking it has a capital-T Truth. And it is this kind of we-identity that starts invading one's private thoughts, judges one's private thoughts, and makes privacy a public issue.

There is, then, a clear theoretical need in Rorty's account for negative solidarity—for there not to be a notion of a positive shared project. There is, as well, a biographical reasoning, and in what follows, I discuss this.

In "Trotsky and the Wild Orchids," we get glimpses of the sorts of things Rorty has woven into his own world, the kinds of honest human concerns he has, and has had, that have been made public in his writing and that have been savaged by critics. Though he has tried to make a virtue out of the abuse, the pain still comes through in places, especially if smugness is supposed to be indicative of pain.[2] Rorty opens the essay:

> If there is anything to the idea that the best intellectual position is one equidistant from the right and from the left, I am doing very nicely. I am often cited by conservative culture warriors as one of the relativistic, irrationalist, deconstructing, sneering, smirking

intellectuals whose writings are weakening the moral
fiber of the young. (Rorty 1993, 31)

In demonstrating his distance from the right, Rorty does two
things. First, he shows just how abusive his critics are and thus
how much abuse a public ironist will have to take, and second,
he tacitly likens himself to that most famous public ironist and
corrupter of the young—Socrates. Though his philosophical
instinct is to distance himself from the Socratic tradition, his
social instinct is to show similarities. Public ironists take abuse,
and even die, in the name of irony.

Rorty goes on to detail the charges of the left—that he is
elitist, a yuppie sympathizer, and complacent (Rorty 1993, 32).
Thus he shows that he is as far from the left as he is from the
right. It seems that no one likes Rorty very much. But at least
these people take him seriously enough to hurl insults. There is
another group that does not. He writes:

> I am sometimes told, by exasperated people on both
> sides, that my views are so weird as to be merely
> frivolous. They suspect that I will say anything to get
> a gasp, that I am just amusing myself by contradict-
> ing everybody else. This hurts. (Rorty 1993, 33)

Not only does Rorty admit to feeling pain, he also identifies the
most salient feature of his woven world. He wants to be taken
seriously, and some people do not take him seriously.

In this essay, Rorty details the two strands of his experience
that develop into his public-private dichotomy. He is the son of
two well-connected leftists and by age twelve he "knew that the
point of being human was to spend one's life fighting social
injustice" (Rorty 1993, 35). This is certainly a serious concern.

In the next paragraph, he discusses the second strand. He
writes that he "also had private, weird, snobbish, incommunicable interests" which included writing to the Dalai Lama who
was the same age and knowing the details of the wild orchids
that grew near his parents' mountain home. He writes,

Looking back, I suspect that there was a lot of sublimated sexuality involved (orchids being a notoriously
sexy sort of flower), and that my desire to learn all
there was to know about orchids was linked to my
desire to understand all the hard words in Krafft-Ebing.
(Rorty 1993, 35)

(Rorty's interest in Krafft-Ebing's *Psychopathia Sexualis* competes
with his interest in the texts of the Dewey Commission of Inquiry into the Moscow Trials [Rorty 1993, 33–34]).

Rorty sets up the tension between the public and private,
and there is much to be said about the particular way he constructs this tension. His public commitment to justice is strong
and commendable, and is reinforced by his upbringing. But he
has problems with the demands for single-mindedness that the
most committed people make. He writes:

I was uneasily aware, however, that there was something a bit dubious about this esotericism—this interest in socially useless flowers. I had read (in the vast
amount of spare time given to a clever, snotty, nerdy
only child) bits of *Marius the Epicurean* and also bits of
Marxist criticism of Pater's aestheticism. I was afraid
that Trotsky (whose *Literature and Revolution* I had
nibbled on) would not have approved of my interest
in orchids. (Rorty 1993, 35–36)

Rorty's interest and commitment to righting wrongs stops
at the door to his private interest in the eight-year-old Dalai
Lama and his interest in sex. One of the results of this separation is that he feels guilty when he takes time away from the
war on injustice. The orchids are "socially useless," the Dalai
Lama letter is "weird," and Trotsky (a father figure no doubt)
would have disapproved.

The way to rid himself of the guilt is to create a wall of
separation between the public and the private, and to make the
private sphere large enough to contain all the "private, weird,

snobbish, incommunicable interests" that people have (Rorty 1993, 35).

The public sphere shrinks as the private sphere grows. And once Rorty says that the "basic institutions" of our society probably do not need to be replaced, the public sphere shrivels up almost entirely (Rorty 1990b, 229). We are left with a public responsibility to vote for the politicians who will minimize cruelty.

One cannot ignore Rorty's parenthetical phrase "in the vast amount of spare time given to a clever, snotty, nerdy only child." This self-description suggests that Rorty is seeing himself from the outside. None of these terms is complimentary, none suggests easy sociability, and the fact that he was an only child who had a vast amount of spare time for constructing private inner worlds suggests that his desire for a large private sphere and a small public one has an autobiographical basis.

If we see Rorty as a person with a strong social conscience but with few social skills, we do not have to think too hard about why he wants to trust our basic institutions so that he does not have to be directly involved in the social sphere. We can also see that Rorty's worry about humiliation might well come from the guilt and shame he felt over being impassioned by Krafft-Ebing and wild orchids rather than by Trotsky. Rorty writes:

> The latter ["accepting your finitude"] means, among other things, accepting that what matters most to you may well be something that may never matter much to most people. Your equivalent of my orchids may seem weird, merely idiosyncratic, to practically everybody else. But that is no reason to be ashamed of, or downgrade, or try to slough off, your Wordsworthian moments, your lover, your family, your pet, your favorite lines of verse, or your quaint religious faith. There is nothing sacred about universality that makes the shared automatically better than the unshared.

> What you can get everybody to agree to (the univer-
> sal) merits no automatic privilege over what you can-
> not (the idiosyncratic). (Rorty 1993, 42–43)

In this passage, Rorty firms up the real bifurcation of the public and the private. The public realm is the place for consensus, for shared meaning, and for the judging of one another. But these rules are not to be applied to the private and are not to be used to devalue the private. We are not to judge one another's idio-syncrasies, but merely to accept them. We are not to inflict shame or humiliation on one another over our private worlds. And perhaps most important, no commitment to justice need be squared with a commitment to say, learning about wild or-chids. Since we need not square these, we need not inflict shame on ourselves, and we need not feel guilty.

The question still remains, however, about how to delin-eate the private from the public.[3] As Thomas McCarthy notes, "Writing belongs, of course, to the public sphere" and so theo-rists need to guard what they write, need to censor themselves, if the concern is that certain kinds of writing are socially dan-gerous (McCarthy 1990, 365). But if the concern is reduced to a worry over the author's own potential for being humiliated, then this need for self-censoring becomes a personal issue and not a political one.

Hall also expresses a concern about the status of irony and its relationship to writing and reading. Hall writes:

> Were one to accuse Rorty, as I am, of humiliating the authors of the books which he dismisses or gives a strong misreading, he would defend himself by say-ing that he is not aiming at the concrete historical individual but the persona created by the books. . . .
>
> But surely there is a problem here. The private individual is contrasted with the books he writes. Are the books his public personage? If so, do Rorty's strong misreadings constitute public uses of irony? Further, if

the writers ... are in quest of private perfection, then the selves that Rorty attacks are the selves they wish to be in private, and he is guilty of making light of them in public. (Hall, 141)

The issue here is less the status of irony than it is the odd notion that the private sphere can include writing and reading. These are public acts and so must be unironic to suit Rorty's need to keep irony and its inherent cruelty private.

Another way of looking at the delineation issue is that Rorty's passionate interests in orchids and sex are really public in that everyone has access to wild orchids, and everyone has thoughts about sex. To make this cathexis seem so private and shameful while still writing essays about it is to do exactly what Foucault says we do with sex—we do not repress it, we talk about it endlessly. Rorty's desire for liberation from the judgment of others, from the gaze of others, from having to define himself for others, runs smack into his writing about himself.

What we need to do here is to determine the status of liberation for Rorty. Rorty writes:

Many passages in Foucault ... exemplify what Bernard Yack has called the "longing for total revolution," and the "demand that our autonomy be embodied in our institutions." It is precisely this sort of yearning which I think should, among citizens of a liberal democracy, be reserved for private life. The sort of autonomy which self-creating ironists like Nietzsche, Derrida, or Foucault seek is not the sort of thing that *could* be embodied in social institutions. Autonomy is not something which all human beings have within them and which society can release by ceasing to repress them. It is something which certain particular human beings hope to attain by self-creation, and which a few actually do. (Rorty 1989, 65)

If we can take autonomy to be the liberation of one's private projects from the gaze and the judgment of the public sphere, then it is clear that Rorty, following Yack, is right that no political/public institution can embody autonomy. All that political institutions can do is leave the private sphere to its own devices, and correlatively, the private sphere must guard against territorial hegemony, or risk self-destruction.

What we need to ask at this point is whether autonomy really is negative freedom, freedom from the gaze of the public. If we look at the sort of public institutions that Rorty commends, and we consider how we are to arrive at consensus, we will see the positive and negative moments so thoroughly embedded in one another that we will not be able to tease out any specifically Rortian conception of autonomy.

Rorty notes that his defense of ironism "turns on making a firm distinction between the private and the public" (Rorty 1989, 83). The public side is concerned with convincing other people to change their vocabularies, and the liberal merely demands that this be done with persuasion rather than with force (Rorty 1989, 84). At this point, Rorty needs to explain what persuasion is, and this he does by saying that "we shall call 'true' or 'good' whatever is the outcome of free discussion— that if we take care of political freedom, truth and goodness will take care of themselves" (Rorty 1989, 84).

The notion that there can be free discussion does not make sense if freedom means simply "free from the gaze of the public," for this discussion is precisely a function of the public, and is always in the public eye. Since Rorty rejects any notion of ideology because "ideology" suggests that there is some underlying truth to be found, it becomes difficult to give a coherent reading of "free discussion."[4] He writes:

> "Free discussion" here does not mean "free from ideology," but simply the sort which goes on when the press, the judiciary, the elections, and the universities are free, social mobility is frequent and rapid, literacy

is universal, higher education is common, and peace
and wealth have made possible the leisure necessary
to listen to lots of different people and think about
what they say. (Rorty 1989, 84)

The purpose of all of this public freedom is to let people
"work out their private salvations, create their private self-
images, reweave their webs of belief and desire in the light of
whatever new people and books they happen to encounter"
(Rorty 1989, 85). It seems as if the only purpose for there even
being a public space is to define the boundaries of the private
space. Thus, institutions, positive by definition, exist only to be
negated in private life. Experience in the world, positive by
definition, exists only to be woven into webs of private meaning. Others and otherness are instrumental, experimental curi-
osities to be experienced and then used privately. Rortian
self-creation is a negation of others, is antisocial, is friendless,
and is, indeed cruel.

Rorty continues the passage cited above:

In such an ideal society, discussion of public affairs
will revolve around (1) how to balance the needs for
peace, wealth, and freedom when conditions require
that one of these goals be sacrificed to one of the
others and (2) how to equalize opportunities for self-
creation and then leave people alone to use, or neglect, their opportunities. (Rorty 1989, 85)

But this passage makes it clear that the public sphere is charged
with heavy responsibilities, and is not simply the positive alternative to negative privacy. Publicly, we must do things, weigh
things, make trade-offs, value others and otherness, provide
opportunity for growth and development. In short, we must be
moral, or to use Rorty's language, we must feel human solidarity
based on our shared potential for pain. And here, we come full
circle back to shared pain and Rorty's autobiography.

Pain has an important function in analytic philosophy that Rorty carries over to his hybrid theorizing. Pain is private in that no one can really feel someone else's pain, but it is also public in that it gives rise to observable pain behavior. By transforming private experience into public and observable behavior, pain takes the individual from solipsism to social construction. At the level of socially observed behavior, pain becomes a kind of transcendental subjectivity. That is, though the particular feeling is valid only for the hurt individual, the social behavior is valid for all observers, is believed, and makes the observers reflect on their own pain. Pain, then, crosses the boundary from private to public, from individual to community, from apathy to sympathy to empathy.

Rorty's public realm is the place in which we create institutions that are charged with minimizing pain. Thus, the one public and positive and collective project that Rorty gives us stems not from a positive/creative urge, but rather from a negative fear of destruction.

Assuming that we are capable of relegating pain to the public sphere, we need to ask if this is indeed what we ought to be doing, or if it is what we want to be doing. That is, do we want to make ourselves into the equivalent of snotty, nerdy, only children who have vast amounts of spare time to read and observe the adults around us? So many other models of sociality are possible, but are never discussed by Rorty.

For example, what if our model were a family of twelve children whose members never had privacy and never expected to have privacy and did not mind telling their big brothers and sisters about sex and orchids? Is self-creation necessarily negative, private, ironic, and cruel? Or is it so only when one has no idea how to share or play with others?

Clearly, Rorty feels that it is crucial to have politically incorrect space. He wants us to read books because we can as easily return them to libraries as we can sit up all night long utterly engrossed. We are not responsible to books the way we are to friends, lovers, children, and even strangers. But he wants this responsibility off his individual back and on the backs of the collective as institutionally represented. No one person need be responsible for any other one person, and so Rorty can read Krafft-Ebing more passionately than he reads Trotsky. And he does not have to feel guilty. Because we have a free press, a free judiciary, and universal literacy. And besides, he voted for the Democrat in the last election.

FOUR

In Between Circus Freaks
and Dead Fathers

Harold Bloom, the originator of Rorty's Romantic hero, the "strong poet," writes at the beginning of his book *Anxiety of Influence*:

> My concern is only with strong poets, major figures with the persistence to wrestle with their strong precursors, even to death. Weaker talents idealize; figures of capable imagination appropriate for themselves. But nothing is got for nothing, and self-appropriation involves the immense anxieties of indebtedness, for what strong maker desires the realization that he has failed to create himself? (Bloom, 5)

I will discuss this passage in terms of five philosophical or theoretical outlooks as represented by specific theorists, with an eye toward explicating, critiquing, and correcting Rorty's use of the image of the strong poet.

Dialectics

Bloom's use of the phrase "even to death" is clearly reminiscent of the precursor to the master/slave dialectic in Hegel's

Phenomenology of Spirit. This battle to the death comes about because each of the self-conscious beings wants to be the one who dictates truth to the other. There are several mistakes, though not yet misprisions, during the master/slave dialectic in the *Phenomenology*, which bring about this terrible battle. These mistakes include: determinate rather than relational thinking; reactionary rather than communal response to pain; and a destructive rather than poetic impulse toward otherness. These mistakes are honest ones because they occur logically, temporally, and spatially before feeling. To the extent to which Rorty makes similar mistakes, he is guilty of misprision, for there is no sense of "before" that can be applied to Rorty's work, but more on this later.

Determinate thinking is that which makes Hegel's self-conscious beings undialectical. That is, the self-conscious beings do not see that the particular and the universal are differentiated moments within the logic of language. Each being is only a particular but wishes not to be merely a particular, for to be such is to be determinate, finite, and fully conceptualized. What the self-conscious being desires is to determinately conceptualize the other, while itself being indeterminate. Just as Bloom's strong poet wants to show how he himself is infinitely a man of genius while all his precursors are finite and failed, so the conscious being for Hegel wants to determine the other and yet remain free and unconceptualized.

There are problems with this desire to control without being controlled. First, the similarities between the two beings are pointed. Hegel writes,

> Now, this movement of self-consciousness in relation to another self-consciousness has in this way been represented as the action of *one* self-consciousness, but this action of the one has itself the double significance of being both its own action and the action of the other as well. (Hegel, Section 182)

They both want the same things, but they have neither the means to adjudicate their differences, nor the emotional sophistication to realize that they can come up with a new way of thinking so that they can extricate themselves. Second, the extent to which each desires to control is equally the extent to which each fails to see value in the other and hence value in the self. Hegel writes, "Thus the action has a double significance not only because it is directed against itself as well as against the other, but also because it is indivisibly the action of one as well as of the other" (Hegel, Section 183). That is, at this point in the *Phenomenology*, murder is suicide, the self is the other, public and private are as yet undifferentiated.

Without adjudication or transcendent vision—that is, without the social and the emotional—the two beings have only brute force. They are, as it were, bodies without minds. Without a sense of otherness as both other and the same—that is without obligation and what Bloom calls the "anxieties" of this obligation—the two beings have no stake in one another's continued existence. The result is the battle to the death. Hegel writes,

> Death certainly shows that each staked his life and held it of no account, both in himself and in the other. . . . They put an end to their consciousness . . . they put an end to themselves, and are done away with as *extremes* wanting to be *for themselves*, or to have an existence of their own. (Hegel, Section 188)

The death of the other shows the other to be determinate, and the one to be still indeterminate. The one is the man of seeming genius whose triumphant body is idealized as a triumphant mind, and the other is shown to have been mindless all along.

The problem with the death of the other, however, is that there is no one left to appreciate the genius of the one. There is no audience, no applause, no adulation. Narcissus may have been happy with a mirror, but for Hegel, even self-love requires the presence of another, for self-love is a moment of self-consciousness, and sociality is a prerequisite for self-consciousness.

The desire for recognition competes with the desire to be indeterminate, but the solution is to be found in a relational moment which fails, however, to be fully relational. That is, the battle ceases before death, but only after there is a clear winner and a clear loser. The winner controls the telling of the narrative and so declares himself unironically to be indeterminate, declares the loser to be determined as such, and requires of the loser recognition, adulation, and hard labor. Hegel writes, "Self-consciousness learns that life is as essential to it as pure self-consciousness. . . . one [of the two] is the independent consciousness whose essential nature is to be for itself, the other is the dependent consciousness whose essential nature is simply to live or to be for another. The former is lord, the other is bondsman" (Hegel, Section 189).

There is, as yet, not enough experience of history for the now-self-consciousnesses to be ironic, to have a sense of contingency, to see that what they have been doing all along is changing their vocabularies. Rather, each still sees a necessity in being what he is, and neither is quite ready to see possibility. The moment of necessity for each comes from their mutual dependence. The slave lives only at the master's will, and the master lives only so long as the slave labors. Neither quite sees how precarious and relationally intertwined their existences are. Hegel writes, "what the lord does to the other he also does to himself, and what the bondsman does to himself he should also do to the other. The outcome is a recognition that is one-sided and unequal" (Hegel, Section 191).

Where the slave will come to see possibility is in his manipulation of the physical world, in his observation of nature, and in his labor. Hegel writes, "Through work, however, the bondsman becomes conscious of what he truly is" (Hegel, Section 195). And further, ". . . the bondsman realizes that it is

precisely in his work wherein he seemed to have only an alienated experience that he acquires a mind of his own" (Hegel,
Section 196). Where the master will see possibility is in his
manipulation of the historical narrative. What neither will see
is their relational status. For the master to see this would be for
him to relinquish power, and for the slave to see this would be
for him to seize some of the power of the relation. These changes
comprise the transcendence of the master/slave dialectic and
the beginning of the emotional life of people in a social setting.

A sense of the relational opens the way for the emotional,
and vice versa. The self-conscious beings become concerned with
each other and come to balance the concern for the other with
the concern for the self. But this move we do not find in Harold
Bloom's strong poet, and we find only a trace of it in Rorty.
Before I talk more directly about Rorty, I want to go back and
trace through the response to pain, and the destructive impulse
toward others.

One of the motivating forces early in the *Phenomenology* is
the reactionary response to pain. That is, the process of learning, or of moving through the development of Spirit, or of
coming to be a social being is a process of trial, error, frustration, anger, and finally destruction. The destruction is only half-
witting because the destroyer does not really understand what
is going on, and certainly lacks the ability to stand back and get
a sense of perspective. Perspective, of course, only comes from
experience, and the not-yet-person lacks just this.

The fully socialized person is, qua socialized, capable of
verbalizing the pain and at least attempting to find social solutions to the pain. This shows the adjudicating side of the social—that pain can be ameliorated communally rather than
privately.

When fully socialized people meet and disagree, they talk.
That this does not happen early on in the *Phenomenology* is indicative not of some essentialization of humans as violent, but
rather is indicative of the logical structure of development. It
takes a "thick" notion of otherness to overcome the reactionary

response. This is not to say that the reactionary response is more essential, but rather that it is logically prior to the empathetic or communicative response.

Finally, I want to sketch out the mistaken resort to destruction rather than to poesis. This builds on the previous mistake, but differs in the positive response. That is, the reactionary and the destructive can dovetail, but the reactionary move may be withdrawal as easily as it might be destruction, and it might entail the construction of repressive institutions as easily as it might mean murder.

On the positive side, communication is the precursor to poesis. We might talk over our differences and the talking itself will help for the moment, but it takes actual poesis, actual making and doing to change the structures that cause pain and thus to eliminate pain. An example is the difference between an encounter group or consciousness-raising session and an actual revolution or other political upheaval. Changing the vocabulary might be a necessary precursor to a real change, but it is not sufficient. More concretely, changing the terms from "slave" to "freed man" does not enable the now-freed man to live a good life. Numerous social structures must change as well.

Hegelian dialectic proceeds not simply at the level of thought or mind, but also at the level of bodies and institutions. It is in the creation of responsive institutions that we find the positive and creative analogue to changes in vocabulary. That is, it is the institutionalization of new vocabularies that makes the vocabularies effective.

Of course, the result of this institutionalization of vocabularies is equally the construction of the conservative moment. Once a vocabulary is institutionalized, change becomes more difficult, entrenched interests attempt to maintain their power, and revolutionaries need to be ever more forceful. The hope, which is Rorty's liberal hope as well, is to create such open and flexible institutions that we no longer need revolution.

But where Rorty starts to go wrong is in his withdrawal from the institutional into his notion of privacy. Rorty takes it as nearly given that liberal institutions are within reach and that they will maintain themselves with little or no active up-keep. It is this hope that allows him to withdraw from the public sphere without qualms, and it is this withdrawal of phi-losophy and irony from the public sphere that is worrisome. Institutions by nature have a conservative moment and this conservative moment needs to be constantly challenged and constantly shown in its true light. It cannot be left to its own devices.

What is called for is not determinate thinking nor reac-tionary withdrawal from the public, nor a destructive or revo-lutionary response to the challenge of otherness. Rather, we must see otherness in the light of the intersubjective, the com-munal, and the possibility for shared creation. It is telling that Rorty calls for private self-creation and shared understanding only of private pain. What is shared for Rorty is still a function of private privileged access; what is not shared is poesis.

Clearly Rorty's conception of himself as having been a snotty, nerdy, only child plays in here, but his views need not be reduced to his autobiography. We can get to this point as easily from his liberalism, which makes us isolated individuals when seen politi-cally, and from his technological view of vocabulary, which pre-serves the semirepresentational notion of "better" as well as a modified version of the scheme-content dichotomy in order for the term "better" to function. That is, Rorty's use of an occasion-ally transcendental notion of "our purposes" coupled with a notion of content that allows us to render the judgment "better" gives him the possibility for a public/political sphere that requires little participation and little change. The public sphere's juridical na-ture becomes fixed by the finality of the vocabulary of liberalism, and this vocabulary in turn reifies the public/private distinction. If all that we share is the susceptibility to pain and humiliation, then these function as the transcendent and, as such, further the reification of the institutions.

Were Rorty to conceive of people as sharing the possibility of mutual creation of intersubjectivity, were he not to withdraw from public view at the first tingling of pain, were he to see otherness not as an opportunity for making himself more compassionate but rather as one more aspect of the world, then perhaps he would be in a better position to carry out his project of eliminating invidious distinctions and fruitless, uninteresting and even dangerous projects.

From a Hegelian point of view, we can fault Rorty for his naive response to otherness. That is, by citing Bloom's strong poet who desires nothing more than the destruction of all that is prior, Rorty speaks as if he had not gone through the whole *Phenomenology* and learned the value of shared creation that the development of Spirit suggests. From the perspective of Spirit, perhaps, Spirit looks totalizing, but from the perspective of any constituent, Spirit appears as the communal, the shared creation of meaning. The strong poet does not want to share anything, but then, neither does the master.

Rorty would insist that his strong poet is a private strong poet, whereas Hegel's master is a public enslaver, and Heidegger is a Nazi, but this argument does not wash because the strong poet requires a public realm that is committed to liberalism, and hence the private has a public effect. Further, by privatizing self-creation, Rorty denies the public sphere a chance to change. By calling Mill's liberalism the last word, Rorty makes it nearly impossible for there to be substantive change in the way things are done. While Hegel reminds us that the *Phenomenology* is a circle, that history is continuous, Rorty would have it end, at least as regards the public sphere, at liberalism.

We can also see from a Hegelian point of view, that Rorty's firm distinction between the public and the private is not so firm. He has a sense of the dialectical at times, especially in his sense of self-conscious irony, but he loses this sense when he gets to the public/private distinction. For him to argue that this distinction is firm and unbridgeable would be to argue that books are not public, conversations are not public, and that all facial expressions and off-hand remarks are made only when the microphones are turned off; or he would have to argue that ironist theorists are not to write, that they must form secret societies like the Masons and constantly censor themselves (McCarthy 1990, 365). Either way, this distinction seems untenable.

Were Rorty to offer a more dialectical notion of the relationship between the public and private, a more ironic notion, he might be able to withstand Hegelian critique. But as it is, he occupies an untenable position that carries within its own logic the faults that will lead to its collapse.

Care

Where Rorty successfully distances himself from the Bloomian strong poet is where he is concerned with much more than "major figures." Bloom writes in the passage cited above, "My concern is only with strong poets. . . ." Rorty is concerned as well with all of the people who fail to be strong poets; with all of the people who suffer from redescriptions or from real bodily harm caused by their position in a vocabulary. What I want to do in this section is to use Rorty against Rorty; that is, to show how his admiration of the strong poet undermines his other positions and vice versa, and to conclude that what Rorty should get rid of is the strong poet and not the "weaker talents" or the nontalented. In the end, I will show that this distinction between the strong and the weak is a flawed one, that to relegate some to the ashheap of history is as cruel as anything Rorty wants to avoid.

One of the striking features of Rorty's strong poet/ironist hero is her solitude. (Note that Rorty uses the feminine pronoun for the ironist and the masculine pronoun for the metaphysician.) Given the ironist's vocation as a redescriber, the ironist has little choice but to live in private solitude.[1] Rorty writes that

> We need to distinguish between redescription for private and for public purposes. For my private purposes,

I may redescribe you and everybody else in terms which have nothing to do with my attitude toward your actual or possible suffering. My private purposes, and the part of my final vocabulary which is not relevant to my public actions, are none of your business. (Rorty 1989, 91)

What we need to ask is why the ironist would want to redescribe others in terms that, if made public, would humiliate? Rorty says that it is the metaphysician who needs to posit a human essence so that we have a reason for not being cruel, but Rorty's ironism requires a positing of the private sphere to make a place for cruelty. It is as if he were saying that cruelty is part of the human essence, and what we must do is create a place for cruelty where it will do little or no harm. So we are privately cruel and publicly kind, or not public at all.

This private space—a bedroom, a mind—bears more than a little resemblance to the Kantian noumena as a solution to antinomies of reason.[2] In Rorty's case, there is an antinomy of desire—the desire to be a liberal and minimize cruelty, and the antinomous desire to be cruel and inflict pain. Rorty's solution, like Kant's, is to posit separate spheres and relegate each side of the antinomy to its own sphere. Just as the noumena is unspeakable and unknowable for Kant, so the private sphere is unspeakable for Rorty. To speak the private in a public place would be to be cruel, and to be cruel would be to be self-annihilating.

What is sad about the reasoning here is that the desire not to be cruel seems to come not from a goodness of heart, but from a fear of one's own suffering. Rorty writes that "human solidarity is based on a sense of common danger, not on a common possession or a shared power" (Rorty 1989, 91). There is no hint, in this passage, of the pleasure of company or the enjoyment of shared projects. Rather, there is this strong poet torn between the Bloomian desire to destroy otherness in order to be original, and the Rortian fear of being redescribed in turn. Rorty's solution is to make humiliating redescription silent but still present in the world.

Rorty continues the long passage cited above:

> But as I am a liberal, the part of my final vocabulary
> which is relevant to such actions requires me to be-
> come aware of all the various ways in which other
> human beings whom I might act upon can be humili-
> ated. So the liberal ironist needs as much imaginative
> acquaintance with alternative final vocabularies as
> possible, not just for her own edification, but in order
> to understand the actual and possible humiliation of
> the people who use these alternative final vocabular-
> ies. (Rorty 1989, 91–92)

Whenever a thinker reifies a dichotomy, any idea must be viewed
from both sides of the dichotomy in question, and so I will
consider this passage from both the public and private stand-
points. Publicly, the ironist cares about not doing harm and so
she must know what does do harm so that she can avoid it. This
knowledge must come from "imaginative acquaintance" because,
were it to come from real experience, people would be harmed
in order to avoid further harm and Rorty is not willing to make
the means/ends tradeoff.

Rorty's liberal ironist, then, is morally obligated by her
liberalism to read lots and lots of books, especially novels, in
which characters are humiliated so that she can learn what
humiliates and hence what kinds of public discourse she must
avoid. So she reads a book in which a teenager is called names
and then commits suicide on the last page, and the ironist
realizes that teenagers have feelings and that they can commit
suicide if their feelings are hurt. The liberal ironist comes to an
epiphany—she will never call a teenager nasty names. For as
many kinds of humiliation as there are, and for as many groups
and individuals as there are, there is a book that must be read
and a humiliating practice that must be learned, understood,
and henceforth avoided publicly.

Clearly Rorty is right to argue that this kind of experimen-
tation with humiliation ought always to be private. It would be

a terrible world if we had to drive people to suicide in order to learn what drives people to suicide so that we could stop driving people to suicide. It is far better to leave this to the realm of thought experiments than to bring it into the mundane part of life. But it seems bizarre that Rorty feels that we need to read every word about humiliating people in order to understand the pain that someone different might feel. And it also seems a bit disconcerting that Rorty reduces reading to the pragmatic value of getting us to be less publicly nasty.

Once again, we have the liberal ironist as solitary and private, even as she is learning how to comport herself in public. She sits alone and reads about humiliation and this is how she learns not to call people nasty names. She does not learn from parents, nor from friends, nor even from neighborhood bullies. As a matter of fact, there are no parents, friends, or bullies anywhere to be found. All there is for Rorty is a library card and stacks and stacks of novels to be read well into the night. And there is an ethical duty to read all of them. Carefully.

Which brings us to the private standpoint. What is the private ironist thinking and doing in her room, in her mind, as she reads page after page after page of prose that focuses on humiliation? Since the liberal side of her is checked at the door, there is only the ironist who is reading this stuff. What does the ironist make of humiliation? Does she get a secret thrill of sublimated sexuality? Is she a private sadist who thrills at the thought of humiliating all the people she has to deal with in daily life? Does the ethical duty to read about humiliation actually cover a prurient interest in cruelty?

Because Rorty has made human solidarity rest on susceptibility to humiliation, he has put us in the position of needing to know everything there is to know about humiliation. Just as judges must watch hours and hours of porn flicks in order to "know it when they see it," so Rorty must read page after page on humiliation.

There is a real tension in the status of humiliation between the ironist qua ironist and the ironist qua liberal, which is mirrored in the Kantian distinction between reflective and determinate judgments. Paraphrasing Rorty on Kant, reflective judgments have no conceptual basis and are aesthetic in nature, while determinate judgments involve the application of one of the twelve concepts of the understanding (Rorty 1982, 142–143). When the ironist is being an ironist and is reading book after book on humiliation, I would argue that the ironist is using reflective judgments; that is, the ironist is attempting to develop concepts where there are no pre-existing concepts. For Kant, the ethical is already grounded while the aesthetic is not yet grounded. Rorty's treatment of humiliation as not-yet-grounded removes it from the ethical and places it squarely in the aesthetic. Once aestheticized, humiliation shares traits with pleasure, beauty, and the sublime—things that are not yet conceptualized. As Rorty notes in "Nineteenth Century Idealism and Twentieth Century Textualism," Romanticism took Kant's distinction between reflective and determinate judgments and reversed Kant's valuations of these terms so that reflective judgment became the liberatory and determinate judgment was reduced to "mere conformity to rule" (Rorty 1982, 142–143). There is, then, in Romantic aestheticization, a move to liberation from concepts that bind our thinking and limit our creative possibilities. If the worst thing we do is cruelty, then the most transgressive and hence most liberating thing we can do is also cruelty.[3] By setting up cruelty as a limit, Rorty is simultaneously providing the space for liberation.

But Rorty still cares enough for other people to set limits on liberation. We can be liberated from the obligation not to be cruel *only* in private, only by reading and thinking and fantasizing. And this is the point at which we come to determinate judgments. We need a strong conceptual sense of what humiliation is so that we never err in our judgments that guide public action. All of our time spent fantasizing about cruelty and reading about humiliation in private helps us to inform our determinate judgments, helps us to formulate concepts.

There is, however, a cost to this interdependence between the aesthetic and the political, between the reflective and the determinate. If liberation is the aesthetic moment of reflective judgments, if we are free in our search for concepts and only in our search for concepts, then once we find the concepts for which we have been searching, we lose our moment of freedom. We regain our freedom only in a kind of escalation of the search. That is, if we read enough about humiliation to know conceptually that practices x, y, and z are indeed humiliating and must be avoided, then in order to get back to the reflective and liberating, we need to read about new and improved forms of humiliation. We are, it seems, constantly challenged to escalate the level of titillation in order to feel liberated from the conceptual chains of determinate judgment.

The result of this escalation, it seems, is that the more we know about humiliation, the more we need to read about humiliation. A drug addiction analogy suggests itself here. The more our bodies can cope with caffeine or heroin or sleeping pills, the more of the substances our bodies demand in order to get the same high or low effect. Analogously, the better able we are to conceptualize cruelty, the more intense must be the cruelty we read about so that we can maintain a certain level of liberation.

All of this private fantasizing and reading that we do helps inform our public liberal selves about the nature of humiliation, and helps us avoid doing what it is that we think about. Thinking is a necessary concomitant to doing, and they are clearly different activities, even if Rorty would not want to admit this. While Rorty does not privilege one over the other in terms of truth-content, he is still maintaining a reified difference between thought/private/mental stuff and action/public/body stuff. The bridge between these two sides of Rorty's account is made up of what might be called instrumental or pragmatic reason.

I want to cite two passages from Rorty in order to explain all of this:

> This sort of claim [that a true method has been found] gets made because such critics have not grasped that,

from a full-fledged pragmatist point of view, there is no interesting difference between tables and texts, between protons and poems. To a pragmatist, these are *all* just permanent possibilities for use, and thus for redescription, reinterpretation, manipulation. . . . The strong textualist simply asks himself the same question about a text which the engineer or the physicist asks himself about a puzzling physical object: how shall I describe this in order to get it to do what I want?. . . The pragmatist reminds us that a new and useful vocabulary is just *that*, not a sudden unmediated vision of things or texts as they are. (Rorty 1982, 153)

The difference between people and ideas is, however, only superficial. (Rorty 1989, 100)

First, to be fair to Rorty, the "superficial difference" he is writing about is that when we redescribe real people we have met, we are relying on the contingent fact of having been born in a particular place and having bumped into particular people; whereas when we redescribe texts and ideas, we are setting up dialectical or internal relations of necessity. The latter is theory and the former is fiction (Rorty 1989, 100).

Rorty's pragmatic strong textualist/strong poet is strong precisely in that he or she refuses metaphysical comforts, is able to redescribe, reinterpret, and manipulate, and sees no significant difference between people and ideas. People are as much to be manipulated and used as are "tables and texts," "protons and poems." The dominant metaphor here is one of use. What makes the strong poet strong is his or her ability and willingness to conceive of everything as a potential tool for his or her project.

If the strong poet sees everything as a tool to be used for private projects, then the strong poet is relieved of the obligation to attempt to see others from their own subjectivity. Otherness is reduced to the objective in one's private quest for self-creation. Giving in to an obligation to see others qua subjectivity is to become a weaker talent, and so is to admit failure as a strong poet.

Once again, Rorty wants us to care about weaker talents, wants us even to weaken ourselves to the extent necessary to relieve public humiliation. But he maintains the instrumental moment as the moment of glory, of self-creation, of pure pragmatic reason.

Kant's "pure practical reason" requires us to maintain the purity of principled thought even as we act in the world. No desire, no particularity, is to taint our reasoning and sway us to act as individuals rather than as universals. For the purposes of private self-creation, Rorty reverses Kant's terms and gives us pure pragmatic reason, which operates privately as that which will tolerate not one iota of the universal. Pure pragmatic reason is purely and solipsistically subjective. As subjective, it objectifies all otherness, uses whatever it desires, and ignores the rest.

Certainly we do not want Kant's thought police running through our minds and condemning us forever for having impure thoughts as we do some deed in the world. We do not really want to hear about Jimmy Carter's "lust in his heart," and we generally do not care whether or not Rorty has a thing for orchids or fantasizes about whips and chains. (Although, given the public outcry over Michel Foucault's sex life, there likely is more interest than one would think.)[4] But just as we do not want Kantian thought police, so we do not want Rortian ones either.

What would Rorty's thought police tell us? I imagine they would taunt us with cries about how derivative we are, how unoriginal, how weak. They would make us feel, in current psychobabble, "low self-esteem." There is no way to avoid making public the fact that some lucky creatures really have become strong poets, and the rest of us are stuck knowing that we have failed, that there are people around who mock us, that we are weak in a culture that values only strength. The more hushed up this secret is kept, the more repressed private self-creation becomes, the greater will be the kind of tension Freud discusses, the kinds of psychoses that come from divided selves, and the greater will be our need to confess. But Rorty gives us no place to confess, because, of necessity, the private must stay private.

A further barrier to confession is one's private ironic re-describing of others under the rubric of instrumentalism. If confession functions as a way of accepting someone else's redescription of you, if this is what the process of therapy is about, then to enter into a therapeutic relation with another is to admit failure as a strong poet. Any moment of intersubjective creation becomes such a failure. And even friendship becomes such a failure.

If we take this to the extreme, we can see that Rorty's public realm represents the failure of private self-creation. To enter the public is to accept, at least for a moment, the subjectivity of the other. To the extent that one does this, one negates one's own private self as the solipsistic subject of all history. Not a pleasant task for a strong poet.

The strong poet is always on the verge of self-annihilation in the face of the public. The most likely result of this risk is that the strong poet will refuse to venture into the public, or upon entering into the public, will refuse to be liberal, and will rather cling to the instrumental mode. Rorty's particular conception of the public/private split puts all of the goodies—empowerment, pleasure, sex fantasies—on the private side and all of the nasty things—humiliation, sacrifice, self-annihilation—on the public side. There is nothing to entice us into the public, and only the fear of humiliation will occasionally drive us there.

To conceive of the public/private split as Rorty does with the strong poet as hero to be emulated, is to occupy an untenable position. Either the private will collapse into the public or the public will collapse into the private.

The Personal and the Political

Rorty's childhood dilemma between the wild orchids and Trotsky, between sexual desire and political obligation is paralleled in Sandra Bartky's description of "P." in her essay "Feminine

Masochism and the Politics of Personal Transformation." P., like her presumed predecessor O., has intense masochistic fantasies which she finds necessary for sexual satisfaction. Unlike O., however, P. is a movement feminist and is bothered by guilt and shame as she realizes that she is fighting sexual domination by day, and fantasizing about it by night.

What concerns Bartky in the story of P. is that the various feminist responses to P.'s dilemma make solving the dilemma nearly impossible. It is the politicization of the personal that has made P. feel guilty in the first place, but to depoliticize the personal would be to assume that there is no social constitution to sexuality. The normalization of female masochism is, for Bartky, as political a move as is the abnormalization.

The knee-jerk feminist response to P., which Bartky calls "voluntarism" says that P., can simply, or with a bit of work, transform her sexual preferences from, say, cruelty to kindness (Bartky, 57). Bartky faults this response as a method of blaming the victim. She writes:

> A pervasive and characteristic feature of Bourgeois ideology has here been introduced into feminist theory, namely, the idea that the victims, the colonized, are responsible for their own colonization and that they can change the circumstances of their lives by altering their consciousness. (Bartky, 57)

The voluntarist view, then, is largely responsible for the guilt that P., and by extension, Rorty, feels. The political sphere is traditionally the space in which there is change. The politicization of sexual fantasies suggests, then, that we should go through therapy, consciousness-raising groups, and the like, to ensure that we have no impure thoughts. Bartky and Rorty both want to make the world safe for sex fantasies.

Bartky, however, sees that the other extreme—the complete depoliticization of sexual fantasies—has its own problems. To say that fantasy is biologically programmed or to embrace, unquestioningly following the lesbian S and M group Samois, any and all content of sexual fantasies is to miss the extent to which social forces might well help construct these fantasies. It is also to miss out on the possibility that fantasy may affect reality. Women who sexualize pain in fantasy might be willing to accept spousal brutality or a cruel world more easily than women who do not sexualize pain.

Because Rorty sees the private as strictly private, he fails to see the extent to which our private thoughts may play out public roles; that is, he fails to see how the political can become the personal. And because Rorty sticks to this firm distinction, he fails as well to see how we might let some private desire out of the bag, as it were; that is, he fails to see how the personal can be transformed into the political. Where Bartky sees a need to cross the private/public divide in order to ensure that we are not isolated in the shame that P. feels, Rorty would prefer to keep up the wall of separation and simply shout to his liberal, equality-minded conscience "Shut up and let me fantasize as I wish." But by silencing the liberal's criticism of the fantasizer, Rorty misses out on what might well be an important source of information for social critique.[5]

Bartky's essay gives us an important tool that Rorty's work lacks, which is the ability to critique oneself and through self-critique to critique the surrounding society that had at least a hand in creating oneself. Rorty's strong poet who makes himself in defiance of all of his dead fathers cannot offer valid critiques of the social world. At most, he can tell us why Nietzsche wrote such bad books, but this "why" will be idiosyncratic and reactionary.

The view that the self can be seen simultaneously as con-structed and as depoliticized suffers from all of the problems that Rorty's critics from the left have charged him with. He ignores issues of power and work; he neglects the good things feminism and Marxism have done; and he constructs dualisms even as he argues against them. Construction *ex nihilo* would perhaps be apolitical, but only under certain circumstances. But as feminists have pointed out, the glorification of matricide (and even of patricide) is not without political ramifications.

We must ask, then, if the effort to construct oneself falls under the rubric of something like work and hence is as political as any work issue would be. By way of getting to this point, I want again to discuss Rorty's self-congratulatory statement that "If there is anything to the idea that the best intellectual position is one equidistant from the right and from the left, I am doing very nicely" (Rorty 1993, 31).

One issue that clearly separates the left from the right is that of the parameters of the political and the nonpolitical. By "political" I mean that which is to be subjected to public adjudication. By "nonpolitical," I mean that which is not juridical in nature, but rather is either foundational and so assumed, or is too trivial to be bothered with. In general, the left wants to extend the notion of the political in all sorts of directions so that, for example, the status of private property, of truth (or Truth), and of identity, all become issues to be dealt with publicly. The right, in contrast, generally wants to minimize the field of the public and maximize that of the private. To this end, the right sees most human relationships as private affairs that should not be subject to the juridical except when doing so will actually and even paradoxically help maintain their very privacy. Thus, there are laws that govern the disposition of property so that the transfer is not subject to public debate, even if the creation of the laws is a public event.

Even from this fairly truncated discussion, we can see how messy the divide between left and right, public and private, turns out to be. The right-wing desire to control issues of sexuality seemingly flies in the face of its desire to grant broad private freedoms; and the left-wing desire to let people have whatever kind of sex they want seemingly flies in the face of the left's desire to politicize the personal.

That Rorty is criticized from both the left and the right is more likely a sign that neither the left nor the right follows an entirely consistent program, than it is that Rorty has found "the best intellectual position," for Rorty's position is as inconsistent as are the left's and the right's positions.

More specifically, Rorty's attempt to refine the public/private split so that it is neither left nor right fails to be consistent on at least the following grounds: (1) Rorty's anti-essentialism would seem to politicize issues of identity-formation, but it is precisely these issues that he wants depoliticized. The making of a self is inherently a political process and it is precisely this making that anti-essentialism argues for, but Rorty wants this making to be a private ironic act. Clearly there is a contradiction here. (2) Rorty's oft-professed intolerance of cruelty is contradicted by his Romantic sensibility that calls for, at minimum, symbolic acts of cruelty to further private aims. (3) Rorty faults leftists for sticking with the nineteenth-century notion of ideology, but then he adopts a position that is still fairly close to that of ideology. That is, ideology rests on an epistemology that says that things can be gotten right, and a teleology that says that they *will* be gotten right. What Rorty does is to say that "our purposes" guide our actions, and even if our purposes change over time, they still act as a framework in any one temporal spot, and so at any one temporal spot, one can be mistaken either about our purposes, or about which actions will best bring about the realization of our purposes. Rorty thus maintains a kind of teleology and a kind of ideology and thus has a moment of Marxism even while he denies any such thing.

If we allow for both Rorty's perspectivism and for some notion of vocabulary change, then perhaps we could clear him of charges of inconsistency on the grounds that he is inconsistent only from some old standpoint, but once we are completely immersed in his new vocabulary, the inconsistencies will disappear. To clear him in this manner would mean that his work is not internally inconsistent, but is inconsistent only with respect to, say Marxism or Straussianism. But, on looking back at the charges above, it would seem that this task will not work because the inconsistencies really are internal. Further, I would argue, once again, the inconsistencies come from the way he divides up the public and the private, from the fact that he maintains that self-creation must be kept private.

In "Two Cheers for the Cultural Left," Rorty criticizes the "cultural left" for an overriding concern with "doctrinal purity" and for thinking "they have done something politically useful if they have deconstructed a text, or detected a totalization at work in it, or shown, in the manner of de Man, the impossibility of reading it" (Rorty 1990b, 231–232).[6]

Certainly the left, and the right as well, are overly concerned with issues of purity and right thinking. We all know the extent to which the charge of "political correctness" has a moment of truth all the way across the political spectrum. And we also know that there are lots and lots of university professors who call themselves Marxists, who make huge salaries and live comfortable lives free of menial labor, and who assuage their guilt by arguing that their work is "political" even if their only contact with menial labor comes when they have to decide whether or not to tip.

But these types, really, are caricatures designed to cover up a much more important issue that Rorty wants to treat as an assumption. That is, Rorty wants us to assume that reading is a private, rather than a political, act. Admittedly, reading is not political in the way that blowing up bridges or housing the homeless is political, but then not all that is political is the stuff of high drama. Nor is all that is political "interesting," "new," or compelling.

Rorty charges the cultural left with having abandoned the sphere of politics because this sphere is not doctrinally pure, because the politics of the United States is, in Frank Lentricchia's words, "mainly unreasonable," and because the left feels pervasively alienated from and superior to the masses. In other words, Rorty charges the cultural left with elitism. Clearly, the same can be said of Rorty, only his justifications are a little bit different. For Rorty, the political sphere is uninteresting, can basically manage itself, and, with piecemeal, easy reform, is getting better and more we-ful all the time.

In Between Circus Freaks and Dead Fathers

Rorty is just not interested in being politically active and so he defines the political sphere in such a way as to assuage his leftist guilt, and he defines the private sphere in such a way as to ensure that what he does with his time cannot be construed as political. In contrast, the cultural left wants to be political, but feels guilty that it is not really doing anything, and so it defines the political in such a way as to make reading and writing the *most* radical things a person can do. If nothing is private for the left, then every act is a political statement and we can all feel as if we have *done* something. Rorty sees the problems with this position, but not those with his own position.

What I want to do at this point is to refine the term "political" so that it can take into account Rorty's criticism of the cultural left and the cultural left's criticisms of Rorty. The leftist claim that "the personal is the political," is highly nonspecific, and Rorty's refusal to agree with this statement suffers because the statement itself is unclear. To help clarify the notion of the political, I would like to distinguish among three basic sorts of things that can be called "political." Each of these functions on a different level. The first is the revolutionary act, or what I would call high drama. It is the stuff of a Romantic desire to change everything all at once, or at least to make a mark on the public and visible world. High drama includes both violent acts like blowing up bridges, and symbolic acts like graffiti-ing the New York Subway System. The two ends of this continuum, then, are defined by the moment of objective change on the one side, and the moment of subjective expression on the other. Objective change *forces* others to take into account the action of the revolutionary and so is always effective. Subjective expression is public and is hard to ignore, but may not force effective action. Blowing up part of the World Trade Center made people stop and change their lives; scrawling one's initials on a subway train bothers people, but they still ride the train.

The second level of the political is the institutional level. Institutions are designed so that revolutionary acts of either sort will not be effective. That is, institutions allow Rorty to feel that incremental, planned, rule-following change will happen over time, and they equally open up space for leftists to say that meaningful change will not happen in our lifetimes. Institutions make Rorty feel as if his own personal expressive life is private and ineffectual—a feeling he celebrates; institutions do the same to the left, but the left mourns.

The way that Rorty and the left define the third level shows clearly how they differ, and presents us with the most interesting difference between Rorty and the left. The third level, then, is the personal level. Rorty wants the personal to be entirely apolitical, the left wants it to be entirely politicized. I am arguing not for a middle ground between the two but rather for a conception of "the political" that takes into account notions of the social construction of the subject while still realizing that the private equivalent of graffiti is not akin to public graffiti and certainly is not akin to objective change.

There are two goals in reformulating the private sphere. The first is to ensure, with Rorty, that there is a limit to the amount of scrutiny one must undergo. One arguably should not be exiled from one's community for having a politically incorrect thought. And if groups on the left spent less time concerned with purity of thought, they might be able to bring about more objective changes. The left would be a better left with some notion of privacy. But not Rorty's notion.

If we take seriously, as Rorty claims to, the notion of the social construction of the subject, then the private making of the self is inherently a social phenomenon, and not actually a private one. If the political is that which is concerned with how the social functions, with regulating the social, then construction of the subject is political as well as social.

Just as the revolutionary level has objective and subjective moments, so does the private level. The objective is marked by experience, which by definition, is social; and the subjective moment is marked by response and creation where response is reactionary and creation is closer to the originary.

Objective experiences include meeting people, forming friendships, reading books, all encounters with culture, and even encounters with oneself such as fantasies, private monologues, and daydreams. These are objective, because the "I" encounters otherness as object, or encounters itself as an object of thought. This "I," insofar as it is a socially constructed "I," is simultaneously the object of social construction.

The subjective moment is characterized by the I's ability to respond to encounters. That is, the I can do things and think things as a result of experience. And in truly creative moments, the I can make things, can innovate both itself and its environs.

What Rorty focuses on is only the subjective innovative character. This is his man of genius, his Romantic hero, his strong poet. But the strong poet blinds himself to the social characteristics that surround this one moment of innovation, and so attempts to freeze the dialectic of subjectivity in what turns out to be an unstable moment. The converse of this is that the cultural left focuses on the social moment and not the innovative and individual moment of creation.

Returning once again to Harold Bloom's distinction between strong poets and weaker talents, we find that this distinction, is not such a clear one after all, any more than is Rorty's public/private distinction, which is intended to bolster Bloom's strong/weak one. No one is strong in Bloom's sense, nor weak in Bloom's sense; nothing is public in Rorty's sense, nor private in Rorty's sense. Rorty's sincere care for weaker talents, which serves to justify his worship of strong poets, falls away once we dispose of this distinction, and so we need to find some other ground for care than weakness of talent. Rorty's sincere and right desire not to feel guilt over his love of wild orchids, along with P.'s desire not to feel guilty over her masochistic fantasies, need some grounding other than a public/private distinction, or a forced publicization of all that is private, or a forced privatization of what might have public content.

The Paradox of Recognition

Bloom's strong poet is all at once an appropriator and a denier. That is, the strong poet takes pieces of his predecessors, mutilates them for his own purposes, and then needs desperately to call his purposes his own, to call his creation his own; he needs to *own* his creation. "Appropriation" is a multifarious term, with its moment of seizing, its moment of making proper or rectifying, and its moment of creating property or ownership. To appropriate is to do all of these things at once.

What the strong poet does through appropriation is to establish a kind of economy based on notions of the appropriate use of property. But the strong poet is in the odd position of wanting to appropriate without payment, without debt, and without, in turn, having his own property appropriated by another. In short, the strong poet wants to be a kind of exception from the general economy, a special case, a privileged elite. The strong poet cannot be a liberal bourgeois democrat; at the same time, however, the strong poet depends on a bourgeois economy of property relations the transgression of which is the definition of his strength. It is only in comparison to the rest of us, to the weaker talents, that the strong poet looks strong.

The economic structure that the strong poet requires is one that allows him to enter and leave at will, which does not bind him in any real sense, but only seems to bind him so that he can feel his moment of transgression. Clearly there is a kind of paradox in the notion of allowing a transgression.

This paradox is very much the same as the paradox of the gift and of counterfeit money that Derrida develops in *Given Time: 1. Counterfeit Money*. Of the logic of counterfeit money, Derrida writes:

> We can no longer avoid the question of what money is: true money or counterfeit money, which can only be what it is, false or counterfeit, to the extent to

which no one knows it is false, that is, to the extent
to which it circulates, appears, functions *as good and
true* money. (Derrida 1992, 59)

Derrida's point is that once counterfeit money is seen in its true
light, is seen as counterfeit, it ceases to be what it is, ceases to
be counterfeit money; for what counterfeit money is, is that
which passes as real money. The moment that it is recognized
as false, it loses its ability to pass as real.

Derrida argues that the gift also follows this same logic.
Once a gift is recognized as a gift, it incurs a debt and so ceases
to be a freely given and freely accepted thing. But if it is not
recognized as a gift, not recognized by either the giver or the
one given to, then again it is not a gift. The gift, then, in a pure
sense, is an impossibility.

The structure of this paradox, which I will call the paradox of recognition, is that once a thing is recognized as the
thing it is, it ceases to be the thing it is, but if it is not recognized as the thing it is, then it still is not the thing it is, at
least for us. The qualification here, "at least for us" is a loaded
one, for it carries with it the whole history of the appearance/
reality distinction and all the epicycles ever devised to deal
with it. It suggests as well that there is a "not us" whose perspective is better able to deal with this paradox than is our
perspective. But our recognition of this perspective would make
it all at once our perspective, and it would cease to be a solution to the paradox.

Before I get too far afield, I want to bring this discussion
back to the Bloomian notion of the strong poet as appropriator
and the Rortian institutionalization of this role. If Bloom's strong
poet can be said to be an appropriator, then the strong poet is
already working within a system of property relations. If this
system recognizes appropriation as an action, even if only to
forbid the act of appropriating, then the appropriation loses its
novel and transgressive quality. If strong poets are defined as
the group of people who appropriate, then we already have a

conceptual understanding of them and so the very quality of strength is lost. To define someone as a strong poet, then, is simultaneously to define away the strength.

Rorty takes this a step further by institutionalizing a space for strong poets to be strong. Not only does he provide us with a conceptual understanding of the strong poet, he also provides a reified social space explicitly designated for strong creation. We Rortians are to have a socially sanctioned means for transgressing social values, and we have the whole public sphere to give us a standard against which we can deviate.

Because the standard is a fixed one, with only piecemeal reform allowed, and wholesale revolution basically not allowed, the limits of our private rebellion against the public are fixed as well. That is, if strong creation is transgressive, then its parameters are limited by what it is transgressive of. If what it is transgressive of is fixed, then every transgressive moment is predictable. It is this fixing of transgressive possibility that allows us to be amused when we find out that some ancient Greek culture critic said "teenagers today..."

What all of this means for Rorty is that his provision of a space for transgressive genius to flourish is precisely the thing that will destroy transgressive genius. For Kant, genius is that which can neither be understood nor recognized.[7] For to understand genius is to conceptualize it, to make it not be other or exotic or different, and so not really genius.

Rorty's desire to fix a place and time for transgression is akin to the sentiment captured by "I wish I could find out her secret, bottle, and sell it. I'd be rich." Once the secret is in the bottle (as it were), it is no longer a secret and thus loses its effectiveness. The private secret becomes public, and as public, as recognized, is no longer a secret.

The paradox of recognition tells us that the only way to have real privacy is to avoid naming it; that is, the only way to have privacy is *not* to have privacy. The only way to have transgression is to leave it unrecognized, in which case it is not transgressive. Rorty's attempt to circumscribe transgression and self-creation in order to make the public sphere safe from irony and revolutionary tendencies clearly fails in its goal to maintain a moment of transgression.

That Rorty's account undermines his own Romantic self-creative tendencies is less of a concern to him than would be his undermining the public anticruelty stance. He states clearly that the public sphere must take precedence over the private sphere and that a welfare state may need to curtail certain private freedoms in order to ensure that the least well off are benefited to some extent. I would argue, though, that Rorty's public sphere is also undermined by the failure of the private sphere to be what he wants it to be.

The possibility for private transgression is supposed to function in part as a relief valve. That is, ironists and strong poets need some place to be ironic and strong, and they will be ironic and strong wherever they can. If they cannot transgress privately, then they will do so publicly, for the value that guides ironism and strong poetics is aestheticism. The result of this public irony is either a revolutionary state, or a repressive state. Whichever state results does not matter so much as does the fact that the result is not Rorty's liberal democratic state.

Rorty might argue that his ironist is not merely an ironist, but is also a liberal. The problem with the argument is that he is assuming that if ironism fails in its attempt to self-create, then at least liberalism will not allow the consequences of failed ironism to be expressed. Ironism is a more powerful force than Rorty seems to think, and it is not likely that failed ironism will be willing to check itself, to censor itself, in order to protect the liberal order of things. Rorty thinks that he can avoid this battle between ironism and liberalism by assigning distinct spheres to each so that they never meet up.[8] But as I have shown in several ways, this distinction is nowhere near so firm as Rorty wants, and the consequences of this lack of firmness are inimical to his entire account.

There is a twist on the paradox of recognition in Michel Foucault's essay "What Is an Author?" Foucault writes about the "ideological" status of the author. The question then becomes: How can one reduce the great peril, the great danger with which fiction threatens our world? The answer is: one can reduce it with the author. The author allows a limitation of the cancerous and dangerous proliferation of significations within a world where one is thrifty not only with one's resources and riches, but also with one's discourses and their significations. The author is the principle of thrift in the proliferation of meaning. . . . We are used to thinking that the author is so different from all other men, and so transcendent with regard to all languages that, as soon as he speaks, meaning begins to proliferate, to proliferate indefinitely.

The truth is quite the contrary: the author is not an indefinite source of significations which fill a work; the author does not precede the works; he is a certain functional principle by which, in our culture, one limits, excludes, and chooses; in short, by which one impedes the free circulation, the free manipulation, the free composition, decomposition, and recomposition of fiction. In fact, if we are accustomed to presenting the author as a genius, as a perpetual surging of invention, it is because, in reality we make him function in exactly the opposite fashion. . . . The author is therefore the ideological figure by which one marks the manner in which we fear the proliferation of meaning. (Foucault, 118–119)

Foucault is showing in this passage the ideological counterpart to the logical paradox of recognition. Because Rorty thinks that Derrida is basically not a useful figure for political analysis, he refuses to think through deconstructive paradoxes in terms of their political effects (Rorty 1989, 83). And because he thinks that ideology does not likely mean more than "bad idea," he refuses to engage in anything even remotely like *Ideologiekritik* (Rorty 1989, 84, n. 6).

The logical and the ideological work together in the following way: the logical paradox, when thought through, shows us that we cannot be doing what we think we are doing without defying some seemingly necessary order. More specifically, the paradox of recognition, when applied to gift-giving, tells us that we may think we are engaging in the practice of gift-giving, but really we are not doing so, and further, we cannot ever do so because gift-giving is an impossibility. For Derrida, the thinking through of this logical impossibility is an act of transgression that we call madness. That is, it is a denial of reason at least for the moment of thinking. And it is a necessary denial of reason because the paradox is made possible by reason and can only be thought by evading reason and embracing madness.

The ideological stance tells us that we are not doing what we think we are doing. Where logic is about possibility and impossibility, ideology is about alternative ways of characterizing action, with the concomitant realization that our vocabulary shapes our actions. Foucault is arguing that when we talk about authors as transgressors, as geniuses, as progenitors of whole new liberating ways of speaking, what we are in fact doing is closing off possibility.

Author-talk, like canon-formation, is a shorthand way of saying that only certain works with certain stylistic likenesses need be read; and they need be read only in a certain context. Author-talk lets us obey the rules of chronology and directional causation without worrying about the madness of reverse causation. Author-talk gives us, as well, genre-talk and so lets us microcategorize and microregulate our experiences.

Another crucial strand of *Ideologiekritik* is that it opens the way for us to theorize about why we have chosen a particular vocabulary. Rorty has been charged with ignoring the issues of power which underlie social choices, and nowhere is this charge more deserved than in his reduction of ideology to "bad idea."[9] One does not need a theory of human essence and things-in-themselves in order to make use of the notion of ideology. One can historicize ideology without also introducing a teleology. In this version of ideology, we would have a method for comparing our vocabularies to, say, our purposes, and we would thus be better able to render judgments about how well or poorly we are working toward our purposes.

Here we come to the thorny problem of whether or not there is a significant, or at least expressible, difference between a vocabulary and a purpose. Are there transcendent purposes?[10] Would the contingency of a purpose entirely negate the evaluation of that purpose? Rorty is willing to maintain that we can evaluate actions and vocabularies in terms of their serving our purposes better or less well. That he is willing to grant this possibility suggests that he really has some notion of transcendence somewhere, even though he denies it up and down. He writes:

> The temptation to look for criteria [for decision-making] is a species of the more general temptation to think of the world, or the human self, as possessing an intrinsic nature, an essence. That is, it is the result of the temptation to privilege some one among the many languages in which we habitually describe the world or ourselves.... But if we could ever become reconciled to the idea that most of reality is indifferent to our descriptions of it, and that the human self is created by the use of a vocabulary rather than being adequately or inadequately expressed in a vocabulary, then we should at last have assimilated what was true in the Romantic idea that truth is made rather than found. (Rorty 1989, 6–7)

But a few pages later, Rorty writes:

> The proper analogy [for explaining vocabulary shifts] is with the invention of new tools to take the place of old tools. To come up with such a vocabulary is more like discarding the lever and chock because one has envisaged the pulley, or like discarding gesso and

tempera because one has now figured out how to size canvas properly. (Rorty 1989, 12)

In the first passage, we have the Romantic Rorty who advocates change for change's sake—or not even that because this sentiment still suggests a moment of transcendent purpose. Perhaps all Romantic Rorty can say is "change," but even this dictum suggests some viewpoint that can bear witness to the act of changing. (I will discuss the relationship between vocabularies and the paradox of recognition below.)

In the second passage, we have the pragmatic Rorty who says that we can maintain a purpose across vocabularies. Rorty continues the second passage by saying that he realizes that a craftsman has a clear sense of purpose in mind as he develops new tools, but that a poet cannot have such a clear view because the new vocabulary is what will make the poet's purposes.

There is at least one obvious response to this admission. Rorty is an elitist who thinks that craftspeople are simpletons who could never invent something without a clear purpose in mind.[11] Creation *ex nihilo* is reserved for geniuses, and not for makers of physical things. And one wonders if Rorty is *publicly*, a committed, nonironic democrat not because he thinks irony is dangerous so much as because he really thinks that most people are incapable of coping without metaphysical purposes.

The less obvious response is that Rorty generally misunderstands the phenomenon of creation because his Romantic impulse blinds him to the not-so-Romantic features of making, and to the dialectical nature of making. Both the craftsperson and the poet, the manual laborer and the mental laborer, are working within a vocabulary. Both have a desire to change the vocabulary in order to fix some problem, or do something that has never been done before. Both invent new tools that are part bricolage and part original. And in both cases, the new tools do double duty—first they help attain an old purpose, and second, they suggest new purposes. Every new medium is simultaneously reactionary and suggestive of new possibility. When Rorty is in his Romantic phase, he fails to see the pragmatic and reactionary character of poesis, and when he is in his pragmatic phase, he fails to see the originary side of creation.

There is, then, a dialectical relationship between creation and purpose that becomes much more evident when we refuse to make the firm distinction between the public purposive sphere and the private creative sphere. Perhaps this is less a matter of a refusal than it is a matter of a realization that the public and private simply cannot be firmly distinguished.

Just as the paradox of recognition calls into question the possibility of genius and of appropriation, so it calls into question Rorty's notion of a vocabulary. That is, the realization that we are speaking a vocabulary automatically brings us to a metalevel and gives us a metavocabulary. The ironist, then, is a speaker of metavocabularies and so is a transcendent being in the sense of transcendence that Rorty wants to do away with. Or, the ironist is mad in Derrida's sense of madness as "looking for noon at two o'clock" (Derrida 1992, 34).

Our inability to distinguish one vocabulary from another is the same inability that will keep us from being able to distinguish private moments from public moments unless we are simultaneously occupying both, or straddling the boundary as it were. Distinctions between any two things are understood as mediated by a third thing that gives us a relationship between the original two things. This, of course, is Hegel's dialectic, which, in its unresolved form, is also Derrida's *différance*—the continuous deferral of the immediate because of the intervention of a third term.[12]

If we think of *différance* and the paradox of recognition as logical conditions on experience, then we need some form of psychology to explain why it is that we come to make choices that are logically impossible. We need some kind of narrative to explain, say, why Rorty wants the firm distinction between the public and private when such a distinction is logically impossible. But in setting up such a narrative, we will introduce our own paradoxes, for this paradox is a logical condition of narrativity. To recognize is to annihilate, to fail to recognize is to annihilate. What is called for is some kind of refusal to annihilate, and it would seem that such a refusal is of the greatest ethical import.

Before I get to what I think may be a way out of this paradoxical situation, I want to look at the Habermas/Lyotard debate, for this debate will provide two important ideas that will play a role in my solution. These ideas are Habermas's notion of rational communication and Lyotard's contradictory notion of the *différend*. I am not looking for a middle ground between these two notions, nor for a reified distinction that gives each its own place; rather, I am hopeful that my solution will make space for each.

Communication and the *Différend*

I return again, and not yet for the last time, to the passage from Harold Bloom, and once again to the first sentence: "My concern is only with strong poets, major figures with the persistence to wrestle with their strong precursors, even to death." This sentence does the work of limiting and situating. The limit is an artificial one, a subjective one; it is "my concern." There is also a temporal limit that is equally a situating. Bloom is concerned with "major figures." To be a major figure is to be already judged, summed up, and in the temporal past. Should one be still alive and yet be a major figure, one has already died in the sense of having been judged as complete. To call a living writer a major figure is to condemn this "figure" doubly—as murderer of his predecessors and as murdered, as already dead. For, as Bloom says, major figures are more than willing to battle their forebears to the death, and so are thus willing to be murderers of one sort. And in our judging of such a figure, in our summing up of a person, we place limits on that person's identity. This is Foucault's point about the real nature of "the author." By identifying authors in certain ways, we limit their power and we limit their meaning.

To be one of Bloom's major figures, then, is to be in a specified relationship to Bloom. It is to have been surpassed by

Bloom in that Bloom understands the qualities that comprise the greatness Bloom writes about. Thus, Bloom's judgment is not double, it is treble. Bloom's verdict of major figure means first that the author is a murderer, second that the author is dead, and third, that Bloom himself has surpassed all such greatness and has murdered everyone.

If we see Bloom's limiting and situating as ways of inscribing himself on a tradition that would gladly silence him or kill him, then we can begin to wonder why anyone would want to be part of this tradition. There is the Groucho Marx paradox of membership—he refused to join any group that would have him. If the tradition of strong poets welcomed any comer, then no one would want to belong. But membership in this select gang requires the initiation rites of murdering and being murdered. One battles to get in and then one commits suicide by agreeing to be murdered in turn. There is clearly something mad going on in this process of murder and suicide.

Rorty sees this madness to the extent that he refuses to limit his concern to strong poets, but he, too, succumbs in his Romantic phases. What I want to do at this point is to sketch out briefly Habermas's notion of communication which, I will argue, presents us with a kind of conversation that is interested in listening rather than in killing; and so provides us with a nonviolent model for sociality.[13]

Habermas, borrowing from Max Weber and ultimately from Kant, traces cultural modernity to the Enlightenment-induced split between the true, the good, and the beautiful, or in Habermas' terms, the "cognitive-instrumental," the "moral-practical," and the "aesthetic-expressive" (Habermas 1983, 9). Habermas writes:

> The project of modernity formulated in the eighteenth century by the philosophers of the Enlightenment consisted in their efforts to develop objective science, universal morality and law, and autonomous art according to their inner logic. At the same time, this

project intended to release the cognitive potentials of each of these domains from their esoteric forms. The Enlightenment philosophers wanted to utilize this accumulation of specialized culture for the enrichment of everyday life—that is to say, for the rational organization of everyday social life.

Enlightenment thinkers of the cast of mind of Condorcet still had the extravagant expectation that the arts and sciences would promote not only the control of natural forces but also understanding of the world and of the self, moral progress, the justice of institutions and even the happiness of human beings. The 20th century has shattered this optimism. The differentiation of science, morality and art has come to mean the autonomy of the segments treated by the specialist and their separation from the hermeneutics of everyday communication. (Habermas 1983, 9)

Keeping this passage in mind, I want to cite a brief passage from *Contingency, Irony, and Solidarity*, and then I will discuss both passages. Rorty writes:

From our angle, [that of us "ironists who are also liberals"] all that matters for liberal politics is the widely shared conviction that . . . we shall call "true" or "good" whatever is the outcome of free discussion—that if we take care of political freedom, truth and goodness will take care of themselves. (Rorty 1989, 84)

There are two kinds of optimism being discussed in these passages. For Habermas, there is the Enlightenment optimism that the separate spheres of the true, the good, and the beautiful will develop both internally and with reference to one another, and this development, though begun in the hands of experts, will disseminate throughout the lifeworld. For Habermas, it is crucial that these spheres be polyglots—that is, that each speak its own language and the languages of the other two spheres, and that each speak to and listen to experts and laypeople. Habermas's optimism is tempered by a perhaps Marxist sensibility that there is work to be done.

Rorty's optimism is of a different order. He thinks that there is no internal language to be gleaned from these separate spheres, and that therefore they cannot speak to one another or listen to one another. There is no internal working-out to elicit optimism. Rather, what there is is what Rorty calls "liberal hope." This hope is that, when people are left alone, when separate spheres are kept properly separate, we will stop doing cruel things. Nancy Fraser labels this hope as characteristic of Rorty's "Invisible Hand" period (Fraser, 96). What I find striking about this version of hope is how passive it is. To suggest that all we need to do is to be fully self-involved in our private projects, and "truth and goodness will take care of themselves" is to make a virtue out of a vice. Liberalism's much-touted individualism is a mask for selfishness. Even when Rorty tempers liberalism with welfare-statism, it is an inward-looking ethic of care. To worry about other people's pain because one feels equally vulnerable to pain is, I would argue, a kind of cop-out, a way of not really engaging with otherness as other.[14]

Rorty's invisible-hand optimism is based on a paradox inherent in liberalism, which is that purely self-regarding actions can bring about social effects. If there is a macro-effect of micro-actions, if there is a quality shift from aggregated quantity, if there is a social dimension to the private, then the claim that the private really is private loses its force.

Further, Rorty's argument that political freedom is prior to any notion of truth and goodness misses the fact that our notions of truth and goodness are constitutive of our notion of political freedom. Habermas is right to suggest that these three spheres must talk to one another and help define one another.

For Habermas, there is more going on than conversation, and it is this "more" that helps us escape from some of the paradoxical positions we find ourselves in when we give up on the notion of "more." What Habermas argues for, and what Rorty argues against, is the continued existence of reason.[15] Habermas argues that the Enlightenment differentiation of reason into reasoning about the true, reasoning about the good, and reasoning about the beautiful still maintains the character of reason. Even as these three activities become more and more specialized, more separated from the everyday, and less comprehensible to laypeople, they still are activities of reason and so are open to philosophical discursivity.

In his essay "Philosophy as Stand-In and Interpreter," Habermas writes:

> Everyday communication makes possible a kind of understanding that is based on claims to validity, thus furnishing the only real alternative to exerting influence on one another, which is always more or less coercive. The validity claims that we raise in conversation—that is, when we say something with conviction—transcend this specific conversational context, pointing to something beyond the spatio-temporal ambit of the occasion. (Habermas 1987b, 314)

Where Rorty has argued that the confrontation with the world, or with any transcendent validity claim, is violent, and that we are better off in conversation with one another, Habermas argues that conversation is confrontational and that the transcendent or universal helps us back off from the coerciveness of consensus-building.

To flesh out this disagreement, I need to backtrack a bit and make a few more distinctions. Rorty's public/private split is meant to address some of the problems here. That is, he maintains space for transcendent faith in human goodness in his public sphere, for the public is the place for commitment and for caring about others. Insofar as Rorty is a public liberal, then, he is Habermasian. That is, he sees consensus-building and the making of pragmatic assumptions about the lifeworld as proper functions of public discourse.

Where Rorty separates himself from Habermas is on the issue of grounding consensus, but Rorty's disavowal of the need to ground consensus on the transcendent, or on a substitute for the transcendent, is perhaps not entirely in good faith.

When Rorty writes, "We ironists who are also liberals think that such freedoms ["liberal political freedoms"] require no consensus on any topic more basic than their own desirability," he is engaging in circular reasoning that, I would argue, is not justified by his desire to avoid the kind of first principle thinking that is traditionally intended to avoid circularity (Rorty 1989, 84). What this quotation basically says when its circularity is made plain is: "We agree that we desire these freedoms because they are desirable."[16]

More striking than the circularity is the extent to which Rorty backs off from it in the next few paragraphs. He starts by saying, as I have noted, that we basically agree to desire the desirable. Then he adds in the clause that this consensus is actually based on "free discussion." He generalizes about the nature of "free." Then he writes:

> The social glue holding together the ideal liberal so-
> ciety described in the previous chapter consists in little
> more than a consensus that the point of social orga-
> nization is to let everybody have a chance at self-
> creation to the best of his or her abilities, and that
> goal requires, besides peace and wealth, the standard
> "bourgeois freedoms." (Rorty 1989, 84)

Not only does Rorty's utopia require the tautological desire for the desirable, it also now specifies the content of the desirable, and so moves quickly away from the tautological and into the programmatic.

Rorty wants to deny that he has a program and so he maintains that he is still at the level of the tautological. He does this by grounding his program in platitudes and in further tautology. Thus, Rorty can say that free discussion means that there are free elections and a free press and free universities; that, in other words, there is freedom when there is freedom (Rorty 1989, 84).

Relying on tautology and platitude as Rorty does is a rhetorical strategy for making what might be controversial seem entirely noncontroversial. Who could comfortably argue against freedom? This strategy also begs numerous questions about consensus-formation, about what it is that enables "us" to come to agree with Rorty that freedom is desirable in his terms. By begging questions, Rorty can say that Habermas is only partially right, but fails by not being ironic (Rorty 1989, 61). That is, Habermas thinks that there is a noncircular ground for the desirable while Rorty argues that a final vocabulary is

> "final" in the sense that if doubt is cast on the worth of these words, their user has no noncircular argumentative recourse. Those words are as far as he can go with language; beyond them there is only helpless passivity or a resort to force. (Rorty 1989, 73)

If we wish to argue with Rorty, then, he puts us in the position of having to be aggressors. That is, either we silence him into passivity, "helpless passivity" even, or we declare war. Either way, we look ridiculous for disagreeing with a platitudinous tautology, and we look criminal for attacking a helpless, good-natured philosopher.

This, then, is the condition of public discourse for Rorty. There is no public space for substantive disagreement, for radical incommensurability, for mutual incomprehension. There is only platitude and tautology.

While Habermas is not entirely dissimilar to Rorty, what he adds in the name of universally shared reason is a mechanism for grounding arguments such that disagreements can be aired without doing the kind of psychic damage that occurs in

Rorty's account. If we see Rorty's private sphere as a refuge from this psychic trauma, a place where one's vocabulary is safe from attack and where one can attack the vocabularies of everyone else, then we can see that Rorty needs this private sphere but that Habermas does not.

For those concerned about not inflicting harm on others, one of the preconditions of free discussion must be a means for avoiding the humiliation seemingly inherent in redescribing others. Universal ground, as Rorty himself notes, can function as a way to avoid this pain. But because Rorty does not go beyond tautology in his discussion of what "free" means, he assumes that there can be free discussion without any universal ground, or some other means for ameliorating this pain.

But it is precisely this pain, and the liberal desire not to inflict pain, that puts the damper on free discussion. One of the risks of substantive political change is the inflicting of pain or humiliation and so if the political sphere really needs to be changed, really needs to transcend the platitudinous, people might get hurt. Once again, because Rorty refuses to make the means/ends tradeoff, he depoliticizes the political, disembowels the public, and leaves us with mere platitudes in the hope that no one will challenge them—at least in public.

But a public sphere that is merely platitudinous, that is so theoretically ungrounded that it cannot even request respect, occasions the cynicism and even misanthropy that lie just beyond irony. Rorty's ironist is someone who still cares, but has no grounds for caring other than her own vulnerability to pain. If the strong poet is the person who overcomes the fear of vulnerability, then the strong poet ceases to be an ironist and becomes simply a cynic or misanthrope. Of course, the misanthrope who, despite his or her misanthropy, still attempts to do good in the world, is Kant's moral hero, and so perhaps Rorty is an underground Kantian in the end. Certainly we have seen Kantian parallels in Rorty's work despite Rorty's claim to prefer Hegel, and despite Rorty's strong anti-Kantian rhetoric.[17]

Rorty's complete antifoundationalism occasions, even if unintentionally, a thoroughgoing cynicism that finds its clearest expression in Lyotard's notion of the *différend*. What separates Rorty and Lyotard, however, may well be that Rorty closes his eyes to the cynicism while Lyotard grapples with it.

Lyotard's notion of the *différend* is his way of grappling with the Holocaust, and even more, with Holocaust revisionism. In defining *"différend,"* Lyotard discusses Pierre Vidal-Naquet's work on revisionism, especially a man, Faurisson, who says:

> I have analyzed thousands of documents. I have tirelessly pursued specialists and historians with my questions. I have tried in vain to find a single former deportee capable of proving to me that he had really seen, with his own eyes, a gas chamber. (quoted in Lyotard, 3)

The problem Faurisson occasions is that there cannot logically be a credible witness capable of speaking about the gas chambers. Anyone who experienced them is dead and so cannot speak, and anyone who can speak cannot have experienced the gas chambers. Because Faurisson's terms under which he will agree to be convinced are logically unsatisfiable, he will never be convinced that millions died in the gas chambers. The *différend*, then, is any such situation in which one cannot speak to another in any meaningful sense of "speak" because the terms in which one would speak have been already defined as illogical or unspeakable. No Holocaust survivor can speak to Faurisson because Faurisson's language has already logically ruled out there being any such person.[18]

The logical incommensurability of stories acts to silence people in pain—victims—in several ways. First, it silences them by branding them as logical impossibilities. The threat of appearing as such is a second silencing. Third, should a victim gain a hearing and a judgment, the victim loses his or her status as victim.

This third kind of silencing brings together the paradox of recognition with a notion of there being real justice through institutional judgment. That is, once a victim is recognized as a victim, he or she is processed through judicial proceedings and comes out with a judgment that annihilates his or her status as victim. One ceases to be a victim once one's assailant is safely behind bars.

A fourth kind of silencing comes about more directly from the paradox of recognition. To have one's pain recognized and recognizable within language is to make it commonplace and seemingly comprehensible and therefore less awful. Lyotard writes:

> Silence does not indicate which instance is denied, it signals the denial of one or more of the instances. The survivors remain silent, and it can be understood 1) that the situation in question (the case) is not the addressee's business (he or she lacks the competence, or he or she is not worthy of being spoken to about it, etc.); or 2) that it never took place (this is what Faurisson understands); or 3) that there is nothing to say about it (the situation is senseless, inexpressible); or 4) that it is not the survivor's business to be talking about it (they are not worthy, etc.). Or, several of these negations together. (Lyotard, 14)

What the notion of the *différend* gives us is a realization of the logical limits of language games or competing vocabularies to help bring about anything like justice. Justice becomes an unrealizable metanarrative precisely because justice for some will logically relegate others to silence. The democratization of metanarratives into multiple vocabularies serves only to make it ever harder to find the silences at the margins because every vocabulary becomes marginal.[19]

Both Rorty and Habermas are utterly dependent on people's ability and willingness to speak, to make some things public so that their pain can be identified and ameliorated. Lyotard's *différend* shows the logical limits of this speaking. Some pains are left to silence, but that silence does not mean that there is no pain, it only means that there is silence.

In "Cosmopolitanism without Emancipation: A Response to Jean-François Lyotard," Rorty argues

> that political liberalism amounts to the suggestion that we try to substitute litigation for *différends* as far as we can, and that there is no *a priori* philosophical reason why this attempt must fail, just as . . . there is no *a priori* reason why it must succeed. (Rorty 1991c, 217)

"Litigation" is Lyotard's technical term for proceedings in which the plaintiff and the defendant and the judge all agree on terms. What Rorty's liberalism is meant to do, then, is to get us all, to the extent possible, to speak the same language so that we can have justice.

Once again, though, Rorty's liberalism depends on people's ability to speak, and this is not at all a given. In two telling passages, Rorty writes:

> The social glue holding together the ideal liberal society . . . [is] a consensus that the point of social organization is to let everybody have a chance at self-creation to the best of his or her abilities. . . . (Rorty 1989, 84)

And further down in the paragraph he writes that

> discussion of public affairs will revolve around . . . (2) how to equalize opportunities for self-creation and then leave people alone to use, or neglect, their opportunities. (Rorty 1989, 85)

Leaving people alone to fail once they have been given the tools for success is the basic formula for Rorty's liberal welfare-statism. But this leaving alone is a double-edged sword. The aloneness might help some people, but it also will silence people who meet up with *différends*. Rorty's private unspeakable realm adds further to the forces of silencing, and makes his liberalism even less likely to encourage litigation over *différend*.

Finally, it is important to remember that the *différend* is as much a logical construct as is the paradox of recognition. If vocabularies can be taken to be different from one another, distinguishable from one another, as Rorty argues, and if there is no one final vocabulary that subsumes all other vocabularies, as Rorty also argues, then the *différend* is a necessary even if temporary condition.

Rorty's way around the *différend* is first, as I have already discussed, to argue that liberalism is well-suited to converting *différends* into litigations, into making the "we" bigger and bigger so that it comes fairly close to being metanarrative in scope. The second tactic is to call into question Lyotard's use of the metaphor of the juridical. Rorty writes:

> But I also want to raise doubts about Lyotard's choice of terminology. It seems a bad idea—and indeed a suspiciously Kantian idea—to think of inquiry on the model of judicial proceedings. The philosophical tradition has pictured institutions or theories as being brought before the tribunal of pure reason. . . . Dewey wanted to get rid of the idea that new ideas or practices could be judged by antecedently existing criteria. . . . He suggested that we think of rationality not as the application of criteria (as in a tribunal) but as the achievement of consensus (as in a town meeting, or a bazaar). (Rorty 1991c, 217)

What Rorty does here is not, as he thinks, to find a substitute for the juridical; rather, he silences the juridical, masks its presence, and pretends that the achievement of consensus comes about without there ever being a judgment made.

A close reading of Rorty finds the application of the criterion of "profitability," of balancing costs and benefits for every move. He does not call his aim "rationality"; rather, he calls it the "pragmatic," "interesting," or the "fruitful." We may wish to wonder about Lyotard's use of the juridical, but we must as well wonder about Rorty's use of cost/benefit analysis.[20]

For Rorty, the use of the term " 'intrinsic nature' . . . has caused more trouble than it has been worth" (Rorty 1989, 8). " 'The nature of truth' is an unprofitable topic . . . " (Rorty 1989, 8). "We call something 'fantasy' . . . when it revolves . . . around ways of speaking or acting which the rest of us cannot find a use for" (Rorty 1989, 37). "The distinction between reasons and causes begins to lose its utility" (Rorty 1989, 48).[21]

There is, in Rorty, as much application of criteria as there is in Lyotard. Consensus cannot help but be more or less coercive at least for those who lack the power to persuade/coerce others. Habermas's notion of free and open communication is an attempt to find a way around coercion, but it gets hung up on the problem of the *différend* and on all of the issues of power that Foucault has raised. Rorty's call for Deweyan consensus, then, is deceptively simple. I want to return to Habermas to help flesh out some of what Rorty seems to be presupposing even as he denies such presuppositions.

In *The Philosophical Discourse of Modernity*, Habermas writes:

> It is not habitual linguistic practice that determines just what meaning is attributed to a text or an utterance. Rather, language games only work because they presuppose idealizations that transcend any particular language game; as a necessary condition of possibly reaching understanding, these idealizations give rise to the perspective of an agreement that is open to criticism on the basis of validity claims. A language operating under these kinds of constraints is subject to an ongoing test. Everyday communicative practice, in which agents have to reach an understanding about something in the world, stands under the need to prove its worth, and it is the idealizing suppositions that make such testing possible in the first place. (Habermas 1987a, 199)

This passage comes in the context of Habermas's discussing Derrida and the collapse of the distinction between philosophy and literature.[22] Habermas's basic point is that linguistic practice is grounded on a need to do things in the world, to argue and convince. Because communication must, at least in part, be action oriented, it must be structured in ways that encourage doing rather than in ways that necessitate paralysis. At the same time, Habermas is clearly concerned about blind doing, about action for action's sake, and so he devises a system for checking action against an ideal type.

For Habermas, then, the language in which we conceive a project is always in court, as it were, and is engaged in a perpetual trial at which it must defend itself against all conceivable accusations. Habermas's problem with Derrida is that Derrida problematizes all language so that paralysis seems to be the only possible recourse. It is this feeling of paralysis, I would argue, that leads so many of Derrida's critics, including Rorty, to argue that Derrida has no political theory and no relevance to political questions.

Derrida's response to Habermas, and Lyotard's as well, is to get stuck on the word "conceivable" in the previous paragraph. That we are obligated to defend our language and our actions only against *conceivable* accusations means that we are not required to think the unthinkable, to listen for the silent, to get out of reason long enough to hear what we consider mad. To be satisfied with the everyday, to desire only to function in the lifeworld, to be, in short, pragmatic, is to miss the extent to which idealization is constituted by practice even as practice is judged against the ideal. Habermas notes that this is, indeed a "performative contradiction" but argues that it is all we have (Habermas 1987a, 185).

Rorty is, to some extent, right between these two positions. Privately, he is comfortable with deconstruction and the contemplation of Derridean paralysis, but publicly, he wants a kind of Habermasian communicative situation in which something can be done. But Rorty's sense of "doing" is so platitudinous and so uncontroversial as to seem even more like inaction than does Derrida's paralysis.

Where we can see this paralysis most clearly, perhaps, is in Rorty's embrace of ethnocentrism. He defends himself on the basis of his conception of his ethnocentrism as being based on openness to other ethnoi. The problem with the openness and seeming tolerance is that it is still a topological or situated embrace. That is, Rorty's conception of "we" is willing to bend and stretch to let other people into the "we"; is willing to say to those who wish to remain outside the "we," "Fine, no problem, whatever you want," but is still, in the end, *Rorty's* conception. That is, the meaning of "we" is largely predetermined, is largely situated, or placed, or localized, such that it is others who must move in order to be included.

Rorty has two sets of logic for this we-saying. The first, or what I call the empty logic, is that the universal "we" is simply the human susceptibility to humiliation. This is empty insofar as humiliation is a negative concept, a fear of determinate negation. It is also negative in the sense that it provides no criterion for differentiation among members of the set. The second logic, or what I call full logic, is most clearly seen in Rorty's essay "Thugs and Theorists: A Reply to Bernstein." Rorty writes:

> The audience I am addressing when I use the term "we" in the way Bernstein describes is made up of the people whom I think of as social democrats—that is, people whose view of the contemporary political situation has considerable overlap with the following eight theses. . . . (Rorty 1987, 564)

For Rorty, "we social democrats" are happy to let anyone join the club. The problem with this full notion is that there is a membership criterion, namely the shared belief in eight theses. By establishing criteria for membership, Rorty gives meaning to "we," but the giving of meaning is simultaneously the exclusion of those who do not pass the judgment. The dilemma, in short, is that if "we" is meaningless, it should not be the term of choice, and if it is meaningful, it is exclusionary and so is uttered in a kind of bad faith.

The extent to which Rorty has transformed "we" into an accordion-like instrument that expands and contracts, all the while making awful sounds to which oblivious people dance at weddings, can be seen in the following passages, one from Rebecca Comay and one from John McCumber. Comay writes:

> Nowhere is this flattening, this collapse of tension, more evident or more revealing than in Rorty's own conversational practices. This conversation is about as "monological" as they come. What is stunning here is the systematic way in which Rorty has managed to neutralize the potentially radical force of almost every thinker he encounters. . . .
>
> Rorty "naturalizes" Hegelian historicism. . . . He melts down the "hermeneutic circle." . . . Rorty reads Habermas as a somewhat misguided liberal reformer. . . . He reduces deconstruction . . . and Derrida himself to a cute little punster. . . .
>
> The "polypragmatic dilettante" (PMN 317) charms all the creatures from out of their caves and toadstools; the Pied Piper soon enough has everyone singing the same old tune. The tune, of course, is the American anthem; James and Dewey wait patiently at the end of every road. (Comay, 128–129)

And McCumber writes:

> I have said that Rorty's accounts of thinkers and texts are interesting, vigorous, and sometimes deeply right. I never called them accurate. The book [CIS] is, in fact, a well-tended garden of misprision. . . .
>
> Partly responsible for these misreadings, it seems, is that Rorty takes redescription as his object—it is, in all its vagueness, what he expects to find texts doing, including the ones he discusses. (McCumber, 10)

The wedding metaphor is apt for numerous reasons. At the moment of the wedding, of the we-making of two individuals, the political context is forgotten. No one worries for the moment about the economic reasons for getting married; no one worries about the legal and religious exclusions made explicit by marriage law; no one worries about the work that will be required to sustain the relatedness of two distinct individuals.

Tradition has it that the woman changes her name, her residence, and her identity so that *she* becomes *we* while *he* is still *I*. This gendering seems to find a place in Rorty's conversation. James and Dewey, and Rorty himself, are the grooms whose brides Hegel and Heidegger, Habermas and Derrida, will change their names. The dialectic is pragmatism, deconstruction is pragmatism; we are all doing the same sorts of things; we all have the same sorts of concerns.

If Rorty gives content to the "we," he has no choice but to bend and stretch texts and truths to make them fit his criteria. If Rorty denies content to the "we," then perhaps it is time to find some other word that neither colonizes when full nor disappears when empty. In the final section, I will discuss what I call a "friendship of play" and I will argue that what this phrase signifies is a kind of practice that answers many of the charges I and others have leveled at Rorty, and at the same time, preserves much of what is right in Rorty's works.

Rorty finds legitimacy for many of his views in Bloom's *Anxiety of Influence*. I will cite two passages from Bloom and one from John McCumber:

> But how can they receive the deepest pleasure, the ecstasy of priority, of self-begetting, of an assured autonomy, if their way to the True Subject and their own True Selves lies through the precursor's subject and his self? (Bloom, 116)

> For all of them achieve a style that captures and oddly retains priority over their precursors, so that the tyranny of time almost is overturned, and one can

believe, for startled moments, that they are being *imitated by their ancestors*. (Bloom, 141)

McCumber writes:

> While metaphors are sounds to be dropped into conversations, redescription appears to be an essentially monological activity. The scientist, for example, can redescribe nature [16 f.], even when she is the only person in it. One can also redescribe oneself, which is, in principle at least, a wholly private activity [27] . . . Absent any conversational context, redescription becomes the activity of an isolated ego. . . . We are again conveyed to the Glassy Essence, now to the solipsism associated with it. (McCumber, 8; bracketed page numbers are McCumber's references to Rorty, 1989)

McCumber rightly points out the solipsistic character of Rorty's notion of the private sphere. But Rorty would not see this as a criticism given his embrace of Bloom's strong poet whose "deepest pleasure," as we see in the passages above, comes not from encounters with others, but from "self-begetting."

In the end, this self-begetting is impossible. As Rorty writes,

> Bloom reminds us that just as even the strongest poet is parasitic on her precursors, just as even she can give birth only to a small part of herself, so she is dependent on the kindness of all those strangers out there in the future. (Rorty 1989, 41)

The strong poet, then, is Rorty's regulative ideal for the private sphere. We cannot, any of us, realize this strength, but we are obligated to set up the world so that we can keep trying. And we preserve the public sphere insofar as it guarantees that we cannot withdraw completely into solipsism.

FIVE

Friendships of Play

Just as the previous chapter contains a close reading of a brief passage from *The Anxiety of Influence*, so will this chapter contain a close reading, this time of the title of Vivian Gussin Paley's book *You Can't Say You Can't Play*. I will read this phrase through the works of Luce Irigaray, Jacques Derrida, Aristotle, Herbert Kohl, Jean-François Lyotard, and once again, Rorty himself.

Paley taught kindergarten at the University of Chicago Laboratory Schools. Her book is concerned largely with "the voices of exclusion in the classroom" (Paley, 3). She writes that by the time kids are in kindergarten

> a structure begins to be revealed and will soon be carved in stone. Certain children will have the right to limit the social experiences of their classmates. Henceforth a ruling class will notify others of their acceptability, and the outsiders learn to anticipate the sting of rejection. Long after hitting and name-calling have been outlawed by the teachers, a more damaging phenomenon is allowed to take root, spreading like a weed from grade to grade.

Must it be so? This year I am compelled to find
out. Posting a sign that reads YOU CAN'T SAY YOU
CAN'T PLAY, I announce the new social order and,
from the start, it is greeted with disbelief. (Paley, 3)

The response to this new role, Paley finds, is that those
most in favor are the ones most rejected, those least in favor are
the rejecters, and that "everyone looks doubtful" (Paley, 4). The
biggest concerns are that people do not want to re-adjust play
styles to include others. A rule-setter (the "boss") tends to decide who will play what role, how many roles are necessary, and
whether or not to accommodate newcomers. The children by-
and-large accept the notion of a single boss/decision-maker for
each game.

By imposing a rule of inclusiveness, Paley is clearly calling
for a kindergarten equivalent of a class war. Sharing the means
of production (ideas for pretend play) with both the workers
and those who cannot work is as strange for kindergartners as
it is for the bourgeoisie, and is met with equivalent reluctance.

I am taken with this notion for a whole array of reasons.
First, it seems quite in keeping with my notion of the work of
friendship; second, because I am the mother of a kindergartner
(soon to be first grader) and I have already begun to see the
groupings formed in her class; and third, because I still carry
with me personal reminders of both being rejected and on occasion doing the rejecting, neither of which makes for pleasant
memories.

What Paley finds as she discusses this idea with each grade
at the Lab School is that the older the kids, the more fair they
think the rule, and the more unworkable. The children all remember the trauma of early rejections and they all wish that
there were no rejections and almost all think that rejection is
part of life. As Paley notes, however, rejection is very much a
social habit with some kids eventually being labeled as "rejected" game after game, year after year.

Paley is well known for her work in using narrative to
teach children. She devises stories and encourages her students

to devise stories. The stories are used both to instruct the kids and to let them express a wide array of thoughts and emotions. In *You Can't Say You Can't Play*, she tells a tale about a magpie, a prince, his daughter, an adventure, a boy in search of his father, a new land, a witch, and assorted others all to show how rejection feels and how it is possible to reach out and include lonely, rejected people. The story ends with reunitings and friendship. Here I want to turn first to the works of Luce Irigaray, who is just as concerned with inclusion and narrative as Paley.

Irigaray and the Feminine Symbolic

In my article, "The End of Killing, the Law of the Mother and a Non-Exclusionary Symbolic," I draw on Irigaray's concern to devise a narrative, a symbolic, in which women can find themselves. That is, the Lacanian symbolic is a language and structuring of thought that is based on the metaphor of the phallus and hence excludes all that lacks the phallus. As women are constructed psychically in a Lacanian world, they are excluded from the system of meaning and language. Women are the Other against which the symbolic is constructed.

In "Body against Body," Irigaray suggests that we think of using the umbilical cord and navel as a bodily basis for a metaphor to found a new symbolic. Because everyone has an umbilical cord at one time and because the umbilical cord is the connection to the mother, Irigaray argues that it would be a universally inclusive basis for a new symbolic.

The concerns here are, as with Paley, the need for stories that valorize inclusion, and the worry about the consequences of exclusion. Margaret Whitford writes that Irigaray is concerned with the lack of stories about mother-daughter relationships. This dearth means that their relation is unsymbolized. Whitford writes:

By describing this relationship as unsymbolized, Irigaray means that there is an absence of linguistic,

social, semiotic, structural, cultural, iconic, theoretical, mythical, religious or any other representations
of that relationship. There is no maternal genealogy.
One can readily think of examples of the mother-son
relationship, enshrined in Christian doctrine and ico-
nography. Irigaray argues that we have to go back to
Greek mythology to find available, culturally embodied representations of the mother-daughter relationship. (Whitford, 76–77)

Clearly Paley's concerns with narrative are shared by Irigaray. In
each case, narrative plays the role of giving voice and place,
identity and power to people. Given that narrative is constitutive of identity, it is clear that the narratives we give children
and those children find and create have the power both to help
and harm.

Let us look more closely at the phrase under analysis: "You
can't say you can't play." The first thing to notice is that it is
the form of a rule and as such is issued by a powerful authority,
an "I" to an other, "you," and yet there is a third party, the
other "you." The I is indirectly present, as is the second "you."
Only the first you is being addressed. What this might suggest
in terms of the imaginary/symbolic relation is that a symbolized
I is making a demand that a symbolized "you" admit entry
to an unsymbolized "you." If "play," here, is a microsymbolic,
a game with rules and narrative and a history, then this
microsymbolic must be open and inclusive. In the various examples Paley gives of children's play, one of the concerns is
what role a newcomer will play in the game. In the children's
world, there is a "boss" who is the inventor of the story and
who knows how things go. The boss, in one case, said Nelson
had "to be a bad Transformer" but Nelson wanted to be a good
Transformer (Paley, 39). Ben did not want three good-guy Transformers. "See, we're not playing that there is" (Paley, 39). But
later the rules are changed and Karl is allowed to be good-guy
number three.

The structuring of the narrative, or the restructuring of the narrative, is often dependent on how much those in power want to dilute their power by including or excluding others. What Paley wants out of her rule is habitual inclusion so that the addressed you and the implied but unsymbolized you are both symbolized.

The implied "I," one could argue, can be seen as more on the imaginary side, standing for fusion and friendship. Yet the I is the authority in the rule, and so is certainly symbolized. What the rule does, then, is to turn Lacanian terms around so that the symbolized I is equally the imaginary, fusion-oriented feminine, the symbolized you ceases to be the excluding you, and the unsymbolized you gets to join in the symbolic. The symbolic, then, takes on characteristics Lacan relegates to the imaginary.

Those who want to exclude, those whose power is story making and who are, thus, purely symbolic, are given a push from the imaginary so that their symbolic realm becomes fusion oriented. Presumably, as the children become habituated to restructuring their stories as others want to join in, they will change their stories so that there is no longer a narrative structure that excludes. Perhaps children will tell stories with "bunches of good and bad Transformers" rather than with specific numbers.

Now that I have looked at Paley's work through Irigaray's, I want to do the reverse. How does "You can't say you can't play" fit in with Irigaray's work in psychoanalysis?

In her essay "Psychoanalytic Theory: Another Look" from *This Sex which Is Not One*, Irigaray traces through some of the major thinkers of psychoanalysis and notes the ways they exclude the feminine voice through both assumptions and failures to ask certain questions. From Freud's insistence on the primacy of the penis and shortcomings of the clitoris through Lacan's failure to interrogate penis envy, Irigaray notes that psychoanalysis has simply failed to include women in a healthy way.

Among the questions Irigaray asks at the end of the essay are, "Why has the alternative between clitoral and vaginal pleasure played such a significant role?" (63). Here, Paley's phrase can take on a masturbatory meaning. You can't say you can't play with your "clitoris and the vagina, and the lips, and the vulva, and the mouth of the uterus, and the uterus itself, and the breast . . ." (63–64). That is, the story psychoanalysis tells about female sexual pleasure denies the bulk of female sexual pleasure and suggests that women who experience nonvaginal pleasure are operating in some dysfunctional or immature fashion.

She also asks "Why must the maternal function take precedence over the more specifically erotic function in a woman?" (64). Or, you can't say you can't play with someone who is like you, you can't say you must desire the same way a man desires, you can't say you are finding a woman who is simply a man.

In each of these cases, the game is constructed by psychoanalysts who allow women to play by only a certain set of rules. These rules force women to negate many of their experiences or risk being labeled pathological. Psychoanalysis, as critiqued by Irigaray, invites women to play, but only through the self-destruction of the very women invited in. Exclusion imbedded in falsely inclusive narratives is clearly something Rorty's notion of humiliation tags correctly as both devastating and cruel.

In "The Poverty of Psychoanalysis," Irigaray interrogates a roomful of analysts who, according to her charges, fail to ask "whether the analyst might not be protecting himself from death by making the other a support of death" (81). That is, the analyst locates his own fears, limitations, and ends in the analysand rather than in himself. Irigaray traces this to the scientization of psychoanalysis (83). Once analysts felt they knew answers and had universals, they closed themselves off from their clients and refused to learn. These universals, however, are cultural artifacts rather than actualities. By foreclosing discourse within the setting of analysis even before analysis begins, psychoanalysis creates what it finds rather than finding what it finds.

In this context, "You can't say you can't play" suggests first that the analyst needs to be open to analysand rather than to come to the session with closed assumptions in the guise of scientific knowledge. Allowing the analysand to play means allowing this person to make rules to define terms, to take the lead. The analyst, then, must willingly cede a certain amount of power, position, and prestige.

"Play" also suggests a life-giving, joyful endeavor rather than what Irigaray finds to be "the economy of your death," or "*your* economy of death" (81). "Death," again is both the foreclosure of discourse, and the talismanic or cathartic gazing at another's tragedy in order to avoid one's own or to cope with one's own (81).

The underlying questions here are, what motivates an analyst to be an analyst, and how does that motivation create a series of analyst-generated interpretations of the analysand's discourse. Looking back at Paley's work, we can see a parallel between the analyst creating rules for the game and the boss doing the same. Both the analyst and the boss decide which roles, people, and meanings are allowed and which are excluded. The analyst, then, is in a position not merely to interpret the symbolic, but even more to create and limit it.

Finally, I want to discuss Irigaray's notion of "gesture" from her essay "Gesture in Psychoanalysis" and show how it also pertains to the classroom and to the function of friendships. I will then conclude the section with a discussion of friendship.

In "Gesture and Psychoanalysis," Irigaray notes that "The patient is lying on the couch, quite still. The analyst, according to Freud, is also meant to be still and seated. He nonetheless sometimes makes a few small movements. The patient may do so too . . ." (91). She notes that the physical positions and the physical movements of the patient and the analyst make "a complete statement that must be seen and taken into account" (91). What does it mean to be lying down, especially if you are a woman and the analyst is a man? What does it mean that the analyst sees the back of the patient's head and the patient sees no one at all, save whom she conjures?

The patient, if a woman, is lying down, physically vulnerable to rape, which Irigaray notes happens "a certain number" of times (93). The patient does not see a face to respond to in the present, she is free to wander mentally over space and time (92–93). This vulnerability and this simultaneous freedom are brought about by the physical positions of the bodies in the room, and these positions, Irigaray argues, are laden with gendered meanings.

She broadens her discussion of gesture by considering Freud's discussion of the fort-da game that his grandson Ernst plays (95). First she discusses the vocalization of the sounds, and then the linearity of the reel on the string. She argues that these are gendered masculine gestures and not at all how girls cope with the absence of the mother. Irigaray writes:

> So what will the girl's reaction be? 1) When she misses her mother, she throws herself down on the ground in distress, she is lost, she loses the power and the will to live, she neither speaks nor eats, totally anorexic. 2) She plays with a doll, lavishing maternal affection on a quasi subject, and thus manages to organize a kind of symbolic space. . . . 3) She dances and thus forms a vital subjective space open to the cosmic maternal world, to the gods, to the present other. . . . (97–98)

What I want to take from Irigaray here, is not the certainty that boys play specific, linear, verbalized games to deal with the absent mother, and girls play specific circular games or self-negation games to cope; rather, it is the idea that the space of a room, of a relation between bodies, of games, is both potentially expressive and potentially oppressive.

If we look at a classroom, or at any other social space, the way Irigaray looks at the scene of analysis and the scene of the absent mother, we may well find that we are making crucial errors in our arrangements, errors that lead to violence, aggression, anorexia, and/or failure.

Some errors are obvious, such as having the teacher always standing over the students, or allowing the most bullying personalities to make the major decisions for the whole class. But others are less so. Using Irigaray's gendered geometry, are the games linear or circular? What sounds do the children make, and how does the articulation of sound encourage or discourage expression? How much motion or stillness is permitted?

From my daughter's first year at school and from my own memories, my sense is that linearity, silence, and forced motion and stillness are the order of the day. The children are forever told to line up, be quiet, and either sit still in class, or run right now in gym. Their bodies are controlled in ways that seem to discourage the flights of freedom allowed in analysis ("Pay attention to me," "Look at the board," "Watch what you're doing" are some of the phrases that echo in the hallways). But at the same time that freedom is discouraged, powerlessness is encouraged. Where you are allowed to be in the room and in the school depends on your appropriate silences and productions. The more you toe the line, the greater your freedom. But this freedom is illusory in that you are always called to the present, never encouraged to daydream or to dance ecstatically. Without moments of ecstasy and absence to punctuate the day, one loses one's voice and memory, one's appetite and desire.

If we follow Paley's rule, however, we find something akin to an Irigarayan classroom. A space in which many geometric forms are encouraged. The children dance, circle, triangulate, line-up, stand, sit, lie down. Many voices and silences are encouraged as well. Singing, chanting, humming, talking are all as acceptable as is silence, and these not merely at recess. Absences become as important as presence. The roll call of "Here, here, here" ceases to determine the flow of the day. Perhaps the children could answer things like "I'm spending today in Bunnyland, so I won't be here. I'll be in Bunnyschool."

"You can't say you can't play" means that the children, and the analysand, need to be just as absent or present as they need. It becomes the teacher's job, or the analyst's, to help make something of that absence or presence. Reading, math, science, and memory can happen in Bunnyland as easily as they can happen in Room 106 or on the couch, and certainly allowing it to happen in Bunnyland is far more empowering than forcing it to happen on a green slate covered with chalk marks.

What Irigaray read through Paley and Paley read through Irigaray provide for my notion of friendship is, first, the idea that a basic sense of inclusion needs to be encouraged early on in life. Were Paley's graduates to write in psychoanalysis, they might well come up with more inclusive languages and geometries than Freud's students have devised. The openness to rule changes and game changes that a Paleyan classroom requires is precisely the kind of openness and reworking that a work of friendship requires. Listening to others, allowing them to join, and refusing to reject are fundamental aspects of the poesis of friendship.

An Irigarayan classroom becomes a space in which the feminine is included, in which absence is made to feel at home, in which voice and body and memory have a place. Play is not restricted to masculine linear games (basketball and other "scoring" games come to mind). An Irigarayan classroom is a disconcerting place for a traditional teacher, just as an Irigarayan session might bother a Freudian; but in each case, the ones who would benefit are those to whom the institution is supposed to be dedicated. Even as Irigaray interrogates analysts' motivations for becoming analysts, so must we interrogate teachers on the same grounds.

Given Friendship: Derrida and de Man

"Play" for Derrida is a broad and complex concept but for the purposes of this book, I will limit my discussion to play as it relates to friendship, and in particular, to Derrida's writings about his friendship with Paul de Man. I will start with a discussion of his *Given Time*.

Given Time is a long and wide-ranging response to a short prose piece by Baudelaire entitled "Counterfeit Money." The prose piece focuses on two friends who are leaving a tobacconist's shop. The friends see a beggar and both give coins. The narrator gives much less than the other one. It turns out that the narrator's friend has given a counterfeit coin. The narrator speculates wildly about the friend's odd and specious generosity, and then realizes that what the friend wanted to do was to give without cost, "to pick up gratis the certificate of a charitable man" (Derrida 1992, fold-out). The narrator then condemns his friend for doing "evil out of stupidity" (Derrida 1992).

The narrator feels somewhat shamed at giving less money to the beggar, though it turns out he has given more. The narrator is at first willing to give charitable readings to the friend's actions—and even almost admires the friend in terms of the various possible readings. Then, finally, the narrator condemns the friend for doing evil and being stupid. We go, then, from shame to a weird kind of admiration to outright condemnation—and this between putative friends.

What the narrator is responding to is very much his own interpretative construction of his friend's action. The friend only speaks twice, once to say "It was the counterfeit coin" to explain why he had given such a large "gift" to the beggar, and the second time, the friend repeats the narrator's words, "Yes, you are right; there is no sweeter pleasure than to surprise a man by giving him more than he hopes for" (Derrida 1992). The friend gives only five words of his own, and is otherwise speechless, save to repeat a sentence uttered by the narrator.

The flights of fancy presented in this prose piece are part of what I would call the "work" of friendship. Here, the work can be seen as a kind of creation of multiple interpretations that must be sifted through and evaluated. The sifting and evaluating are another kind of work—the labor of judgment.

Both creation and judgment are integral parts of friendship. We must interpret one another, but always with Derrida's stricture to read and reread, to read responsibly, to respond to what we read. Derrida's essays on the de Man "case"—"Like the Sound of the Sea Deep within a Shell" and "Biodegradables" are concerned foremost with the issues of reading and responsibility, with the work of friendship.

Where the frontline critics of de Man would prefer to enter the stage *in medias res*, with an a priori table of judgments against de Man, Derrida finds instead that the work of friendship demands the labor of reading and thinking. This labor is not to be limited to one's "friends" where "friends" is a limited notion. Rather, the work of friendship is owed to everyone. This work requires that each of us reads and talks and judges, but without the ease, comfort, and simplicity of a priori categories.

In an interview with Jean-Luc Nancy, Derrida, speaking about the name "Auschwitz" says:

> I suppose, I hope you are not expecting me simply to say "I condemn Auschwitz" or "I condemn every silence on Auschwitz." As regards this last phrase or its equivalents, I find a bit indecent, indeed, obscene, the mechanical nature of improvised trials against all those whom one thinks one can accuse of not having named or thought "Auschwitz." . . . If we admit . . . that the thing remains unthinkable . . . then let's stop diagnosing the alleged silences. . . . Of course, silence on Auschwitz will never be justifiable; nor is speaking about it in such an instrumental fashion and in order to say nothing, to say nothing that does not go without saying, trivially, serving primarily to give oneself a good conscience. . . . (Derrida 1991, 118)

The caution Derrida recommends is that we not give in to easy denunciations, even of things that we know need some kind of denunciation. To reduce someone's experience of horror to a metonymical conscience-easing sentence is not the same as the ethical. This reduction protects its speakers from having to do the real work of being with survivors and even of being with the dead. For, indeed, the survivors have been with the dead before death and during death.

Being with survivors cannot, and must not, be reduced in the Rortian manner to reading all of Elie Wiesel's novels, all of Primo Levi's novels, and the unexpurgated version of Anne Frank's diary. No matter how long the list is, how "complete" or "incomplete" it is, the list making itself is a misguided enterprise. We can laugh easily at Sartre's character in *Nausea* who is reading his way through a library alphabetically. He needs some way to systematize his project, and chooses the alphabet as his way.

This urge to organize a project must be refused. It is the same urge that gives us canonical texts that are "must reads" and noncanonical texts the reading of which is a waste of precious time. It is also the same urge that makes Rorty list several genres and then choose novels as the best genre for doing what he wants done. Certainly there is a feeling of power and of safety in the *pre*conception—the concept that comes before experience, before judgment, and that makes experience and judgment unnecessary.

Derrida's neologistic *"Je ne pveut pas lire"*—I can/will not read—illustrates this *pre*conception (Derrida 1989, 823). That is, the *"ne pveut pas"* always comes before the act of reading and working and makes the work of reading impossible and unnecessary even as it is undesired. The work of reading, and indeed the work of friendship are never given a chance to be issues in the face of *"ne pveut pas."* Derrida's pained, angered, and even resigned call for reading meets, perhaps, with a *différend.* He writes:

> This request for reading (isn't this rather normal? what less could one ask for?) seems extraordinary to them, even exorbitant. What is more, I never said that *it was necessary at all costs to read* de Man or anybody else, but, and this is quite a different thing, that *if* at least one claims to speak about all this, it is a good

idea to read, even better to reread, preferably everything one can. (Derrida 1989, 838)

But de Man's critics, and all list makers, define themselves
through the exclusion of some other. If one simply labels de
Man as "beyond the pale," then one not only has a smaller
stack of books to read, but also one can publicly label oneself
as "anti-anti-Semitic" and not worry at all about what one means.

Here I would like to imagine for a moment de Man, Derrida,
and a variety of critics in Vivian Paley's kindergarten class. They
are told that the new rule is "You can't say you can't play." Does
de Man simply not tell his secret until he is dead? But then how
does his best friend respond to the other kids? It seems to me
that Paley, who wants friendship and inclusion to be automatic,
would do just what Derrida has done—to defend and yet judge,
to be careful, to construct narratives that show how complex, if
unfortunate, the situation is. Perhaps she would write "Counterfeit Money."

Just as Paley turns to the Prince and Princess and witch to
discuss the virtues of inclusion and the pain of exclusion, so
Derrida turns to a discussion of "Counterfeit Money" to show
that a gift is not always what it seems. Story telling gives us a
space in which we can work out nuances in moral possibility.
This is close to Rorty's position, but not quite. He emphasizes
reading, and hardly mentions writing or telling. If we only read,
we are limited by what has been written, and thus we must
write and tell stories as well.

In Paley's classroom, then, Derrida is allowed to tell de Man
stories and the other kids need to listen and tell their own
stories. They cannot simply say "Paul de Man was bad" and
forget about him. De Man, even in death, gets to play.

There is an element here of history, and of the future that
will be history. That is, what is owed to de Man, a place in our
stories rather than exile and a hole that gets hastily stitched, is
what will be owed to each one of us should it turn out that we,
too, have a secret. Paley is well aware of the future that becomes

experience and a past when she notes that the same children get excluded year after year. They become marked by the group. Today's exclusion becomes tomorrow's rule to exclude and it all comes together in a "bad childhood" as memory. Slowly the bad childhood is disclosed to a therapist or a friend or in an action. In any case, the seemingly small acts of a day in kindergarten become a lifetime.

What seems to determine one's history, one's life story, is an accident of just what one's secret is and how it is revealed. Sometimes people's secrets are simply culturally accepted atrocities that are revealed as such much later. Here Kant's and Hume's racisms come to mind. Their secrets come to light as a concern two-hundred-odd years later and we are accustomed to trying to tease out the value of their work from the vile in their thoughts. Scholars who care about their work take on the role of their friends and defend them in the face of numerous attacks.

Sometimes the secret is revealed in kindergarten. It can be as simple as not having a certain toy, or as complex as misunderstanding body language or spoken language. Such a secret, if revealed early leads to a lifetime of exclusion.

What Derrida and Paley both see is that the habitual excluding, exiling, and defaming in the face of a secret revealed is the cause of enormous pain and betrayal. Derrida knows that secrets and atrocities abound, and that denouncing them in others tends to be a feel-good and even talismanic act. I have denounced evil and so I cannot become evil: phew!

History, however, makes room for everyone to become evil, for everyone to have a secret that gets revealed. Understanding this plays a role in the need for the work of friendship. This, not merely because it could happen to us, but more so that we cause less pain in the world.

Of course some secrets are more consequential than others and deserve greater note and greater concern, but we should not standardize our responses. That is, when famous thinkers X, Y, and Z turn out to be full of hate, our responses, the consequences we create for their hatred, need to be tailored, particularized, and worked out anew each time. We need to find out if, indeed, they are full of hate, and just what this means for them and for us. When Derrida calls on us to read and reread, it is this he is asking for. De Man is not simply one more anti-Semite, and we the critics are not merely one more group of right-thinking upstanding citizens ready to stop the atrocities of the previous generation. The habit of easy denunciation and self-righteousness needs to give way to a Paleyan habit of inclusion. And here, it would seem, is a good place to look back briefly at Aristotle.

The Habit of Friendship, or Aristotle Modified

For Aristotle, our moral virtues are formed by habit. "It makes no small difference," he writes, "then, whether we form habits of one kind or of another from our very youth; it makes a very great difference, or rather *all* the difference" (1103b25). When Paley discusses rejection, it is characterized as habit; learned practices repeated over and over that "will soon be carved into stone" (3). Some kids get rejected, others do the rejecting, and once these roles are learned, they rarely change.

If we combine Aristotle's notion of virtue as habit with a discussion of friendship, we can categorize a kind of friendship he omits—one that I will call a *friendship of play*.

Aristotle characterizes friendship as of three kinds, that of utility, that of pleasure, and that which is perfect. He writes:

> Now those who love each other for their utility do not love each other for themselves but in virtue of some good which they get from each other. So too with those who love for the sake of pleasure. . . . Therefore those who love for the sake of utility love for the sake of what is good *for themselves*, and those who love for the sake of pleasure do so for the sake of what is pleasant *to themselves*, and not in so far as the other is the person loved but in so far as he is useful or pleasant. (1156a6–27)

In these kinds of friendship, the object is not the other, but rather the self. The other is merely incidental and could be any other. There is nothing unique or special about the other.

Perfect friendship, on the other hand, has the other as the central concern. Aristotle writes:

> Perfect friendship is the friendship of men who are good, and alike in virtue; for these wish well alike to each other *qua* good, and they are good in themselves. Now these who wish well to their friends for their sake are most truly friends; for they do this by reason of their own nature and not incidentally. . . . (1156a27)

Perfect friendship, according to Aristotle, is limited to men of equal status whose desire for the other resides in the perfection of the other. Ironically, the other is so like the self that there may well be an element of narcissism or Kant's "dear self" lurking about. At any rate, I want less to get bogged down in criticisms of the clear sexism and classism of this model than to take from it what I need for my own theory of friendship.

The friendship in a Paleyan classroom fits none of Aristotle's ideal types. Utility is not the right description because no one is trying to get something out of an other, and the others are not at all interchangeable. Pleasure does not work either because, in fact, children have to put up with some amount of displeasure as they adjust to the system and as they play within it. And clearly, these are not to be perfect friendships between men whose love is solely the other.

What I would suggest is yet another kind of friendship, which I have termed "friendship of play." The goal of the *work* of friendship is a friendship of *play*. Paley alludes several times to the discomfort that children seem to experience when they feel they have to reject, and the relief they experience when they no longer feel they must reject others. The habitual work of inclusion eases the burden of being unfair and makes each child feel better, kinder, and more fair.

Socially, "You can't say you can't play" reduces the level of competition for attention from particular popular children. Further, it ends the basic divisions that breed resentment and depression. The result is a socially cohesive group in which the members are aware of each other's emotional states, desires, and abilities. No one can get by without this awareness, and without the concomitant concern for others.

A legitimate question arises here, one which Paley herself wonders about. She writes, "But can this kind of morality be legislated? And what about that other moral imperative: the right to choose one's companions, unpressured and unopposed? Well you can still choose your own companions. No one is telling you *not* to play with someone" (73).

In the old, exclusive system, of course, many people are told *not* to play with certain people. But in the new system there does seem to be something like a violation of a kind of private space of free association, the space in which to refuse others. An easy way through this problem is to argue that school is a public space and so does not at all allow for private choices. The problem with this argument, as with Rorty's public/private distinction is that it simply does not hold up to rigorous scrutiny. How then do we keep what is good about some sense of space that is not subject to the gaze of others while maintaining what is clearly good about friendships of play?

Aristotle provides part of the answer in his notion of caring for something beyond oneself in friendship. While perfect friendship seems to me to fall into narcissism, a friendship of play seems more truly concerned about the emotional well-being both of the group as a whole and each individual in the group. This is not to say that it depends on altruism because of course one's own well-being is involved. But because the emphasis is not on equality of condition the way it is for Aristotle, the narcissistic element is minor.

My desire here is to avoid the hyperindividualism that confers rights on people qua individuals and that especially confers the right to exclude. At the same time, I want to avoid the converse, hypercommunitarianism, which confers rights on groups qua groups and does not leave people alone when solitude is what is desired.

What I hope is that the notion of friendship of play manages to avoid both the private hyperindividualism of Rorty's strong poet and the overly public hypercommunitarian "politics of meaning" that has been bandied about in recent public discourse. (I have to confess that hearing the President utter the phrase "the politics of meaning" has often made me wish to write "the politics of meaninglessness." Mercifully, the whole thing was dropped because it did not help increase favorable ratings in opinion polls.) Loading too much meaning onto connections between people takes away from the pleasures that are inherent in friendship and turns relationships into civic duties.

The examples of this removal of pleasure from private and public life are numerous. From right-to-work laws that do away with unions, to workfare which, in public discourse, does away with "welfare queens who drive Cadillacs save when they are watching soap operas or getting pregnant for the twelfth time just to collect ten additional dollars each month," to antidrug campaigns that do away with the myriad group pleasures that many drugs induce—each of these stems from a need to make sure that no one else is having fun or getting power.

What is so striking is the extent to which our public discourse condemns pleasure. Even at the level of marriage—some states are proposing making married couples wait before divorcing because the family is the building block of the nation. Getting married and staying that way become civic duties.

I see the friendship of play as a way to get away from this model because it brings back the notion that pleasure is important. Aristotle emphasizes pleasure as a good, and not as something that corrupts and must be avoided at all costs. Clearly contemporary public life needs to return to this notion.

Within the Aristotelian rubric, "You can't say you can't play" suggests that play and pleasure are important components of social life. The modified Aristotelian classroom is a place where inclusive play is encouraged so that children become habituated to it. Rather than emphasizing the duty to let someone play whether or not that person fits in, this kind of classroom encourages the creative play that can change a narrative to let anyone in. We can see a parallel between the need for flexibility in narrative construction and the move to "multicultural" narratives in public discourse. Antimulticulturalists seem to lack the flexibility to change their narratives to let others join the game.

Here is a place where Rorty's notion of irony can be helpful. Irony signals the lack of commitment to a particular narrative, and clearly something like this is called for. But what Rorty calls a "lack of commitment" I would prefer to term "flexibility" because it seems to me that commitment to one's discourse is an important notion. Here Alfred Hitchcock's film *Rope* comes to mind. In *Rope* a professor expounds on the need to kill in order to transgress ordinary morality. Two students take him seriously and murder a fellow student. The professor is left shocked that anyone would take him seriously. He is, perhaps, an ironist strong poet who refuses the mantle of ordinary morality—at least while he is talking.

My notion of flexibility of narrative preserves the space for change that Rorty rightly claims, but does so in a way that preserves as well a sense of commitment. Rorty has a sad passage that shows that commitment is both absent and desired. He writes:

> The ironist spends her time worrying about the possibility that she has been initiated into the wrong tribe, taught to play the wrong language game. She worries that the process of socialization which turned her into a human being by giving her a language may have given her the wrong language, and so turned her into the wrong kind of human being. So, the more she is driven to articulate her situation in philo-

sophical terms, the more she reminds herself of her rootlessness by constantly using terms like "Weltan-schauung," "perspective," "dialectic," "conceptual framework," "historical epoch," "language game," "re-description," "vocabulary," and "irony." (CIS, 75)

What I find striking about this passage is first the intense feeling alienation. Worrying about being the wrong kind of human being speaking the wrong language bespeaks a real inability to be with others, and even to be with oneself. Second, the notion of a variety of languages or vocabularies is not so far from the practice of story telling in Paley's classroom. Just as stories change from day to day and purpose to purpose, so do Rorty's vocabularies. The differences, I think, are first that a child more fervently believes in the stories she is telling and so derives more pleasure and less anxiety, and second that despite this fervency, children are, with a bit of help, very flexible in changing their stories to fit newcomers and new situations. The prodding, for Paley's room is "You can't say you can't play."

If there is space in narrative construction for each child, then the sense of alienation is absent. At the same time, the narratives change so often and from so many perspectives that there is space for social critique and for metanarrative awareness. The children can say that they do not want to be in a particular story, that one child is a tyrant, or that the ending has to be different. They also know that they are telling stories. There is not, then, the metaphysical function of world-disclosure, and yet there is commitment to the stories.

Because everyone gets a chance to participate in the story making, no one needs to feel left out, alienated, in the wrong language. The language is changing and the change is then taken to be normal.

To get back to my final vocabulary to which I feel commitment, what friendships of play do is to make space for stories to be told, for people to feel connected. There is a need to have space in which to tell stories and play out roles. Nearly every woman who has given birth has a birth story she tells over and over; people who rehab their houses have paint and disaster stories; people who have weather tell weather stories. The list goes on. What makes people feel alienated is a sense that their stories are not valued. What makes Paley's classroom so wonderful is that the stories are valued by definition and constitution. Friends committed to shared play listen to each other's stories.

There is, however, a problem with my account. What if someone does not want to tell her story? The group, in Paley's room, cannot reject an individual, but what about the individual who rejects the group? What is this refusal, how is it handled, and is it even something to be "handled"? The next two thinkers I will discuss, Herbert Kohl and Lyotard, both take on the issue "I say I won't play."

Not-Learning and Not-Playing: Herbert Kohl on Refusal

Herbert Kohl's essay "I Won't Learn From You" contains a series of telling anecdotes that show the political potency of refusing to learn. The first is the story of Wilfredo, the grandfather of one of Kohl's students (1–2). Wilfredo will not learn English. After talking to him, Kohl realizes that Wilfredo's refusal to learn comes not from fear of trying or fear of failing, but rather from the fear of his grandchildren's losing their Spanish families and culture (1). From this observation, Kohl learns that "willed refusal to learn" is a strategy far different from the inability to learn.

Kohl goes on to discuss his not-learning of Yiddish at home and his not-learning of Hebrew for his bar mitzvah. He now regrets the former; and of the latter he notes that when he cheated on his final Hebrew test, he not only copied all the answers properly, he also ignorantly copied someone else's name onto his test. The teacher found out and humiliated Kohl in front of the class (3–6). Kohl writes, "I never forgot this humiliation and when I became a teacher, I resolved never to humiliate any of my students" (6).

Not-learning comes about because learning requires an acceptance of a set of power relations, social meanings, and cultural assumptions that can range from the irritating to the devastating. Here Rorty's discussion of humiliation comes to mind. If a person is forced to take on a set of meanings that make the person incapable of reconstructing him- or herself afterward, this is the height of torture.

On the mildest end, I remember having teachers I simply did not like, and I made little effort to learn from them. They had irritating habits or seemed to dislike children. Quietly, on my own, I shut down. On the extreme end, a defiant, angry, even violent child might well be refusing the dominance of the dominant culture. Refusing to learn is a potent political strategy that allows the child to refuse the oppressiveness of the world that the teacher and the class material symbolize.

Kohl discusses at length a student he knew, Akmir (15–25). (My summary closely follows Kohl's text.) Akmir was transferred out of his regular high school because he challenged the racism abounding in the curriculum. He irritated teachers and the principal and to get rid of him, they sent him to a different school. Kohl notes that despite having passed all of his classes, Akmir did not receive his diploma "for 'citizenship' reasons" (16). The dominant culture represented by school authorities refuses to grant admittance to a rebel.

Akmir's story continues. He ends up in a psychology class that Kohl is coteaching at Teachers College. Akmir challenges Kohl with stridency and accuracy. Akmir dreams of writing "in a separated, separatist language, a postrevolutionary language. His dream was one of writing beyond race while affirming the quality of his experience and the history of his people" (23).

Akmir's dream ends when he thinks he needs his high school diploma to get into City College's open enrollment writing program. Despite Kohl's recommendation, the high school guidance counselor still did not think that Akmir was enough of a citizen and refused. This, combined with a draft notice sent Akmir back to his old neighborhood where he died of a heroin overdose (25).

Akmir's story highlights many crucial facets of my notion of friendship. First, Akmir is failed by a school system and culture that refuses to offer him friendship. The often-noted uses of light and dark, civilized and primitive as metaphors for good and bad and white and black, are, in every instance, ways of excluding and refusing to offer friendship. Forcing dark-skinned people to accept these metaphors is precisely the kind of humiliation Rorty finds to be cruel. Not allowing people who challenge these metaphors to have space to re-create language and meaning without the elements that humiliate is a further failure of friendship.

Because Akmir was failed on so many levels, he refused the system. The system had a chance to gain his respect by admitting its failure. Not until he accidentally bumped into Kohl did Akmir get the mainstream respect and offer of friendship he deserved. And because the power is still in the mainstream, strategically Akmir needed this friendship even though it is clear that strategy was not at issue. Even Kohl's friendship was not enough. Sadly, Akmir did not actually need his diploma to get into the writing program. The letter was sent by mistake and Akmir died by mistake.

Akmir had no choice but to refuse the group, to not-learn, until he had a context of friendship. And even in the context of friendship, Akmir's learning was guided by refusing the humiliation of racist metaphor. What the space of friendship did for Akmir was to give him respect for this refusal, and at least to attempt to give him the space to create a new language without humiliation in it.

From Paley's perspective, Akmir's schooling and the language he learned were replete with subtle and overt repetitions of "You can't play." His response was, eventually, "I won't play." His high school teachers said, "If you don't play then go away." Akmir was sent off because the group with the power to decide what games and rules were allowed did not want him around.

I think of Akmir as a small Socrates. Small because he has not yet been given his place in history, his chance to rewrite language and meaning to make them more thoughtful. Before his "hemlock," he found a small space that allowed him to dream, an offer of friendship that allowed him to speak and sharpen his positions. But, sadly, it was only a small space, and not big enough.

I do not, however, want to reduce Akmir's principled refusals to a Freudian early childhood trauma of exclusion. Akmir refused to join the group not because the group was mean to him, but because the group could not include him while allowing him to maintain his identity.

What is at stake with Akmir and many other not-learners is a whole structure of meaning and narrative that is embedded in language and social relations. Akmir, in Paley's classroom, would have to be able to tell stories in his new language in order to be able to play. Just as Irigaray faults the whole history of psychoanalysis for leaving out the feminine position, so Akmir faults Western Civilization for leaving out almost everything.

To teach Akmir is to be forced to unlearn a lot of habits and structures of language and socialization. To teach Akmir is to learn from him his language. Kohl describes the process of giving up racist metaphor (19–20). Kohl was willing, but many of Akmir's other teachers were not.

For Akmir, "You can't say you can't play" means that he has to be able to play in his language and other people have to adjust to him. This is precisely the move that has brought about multiculturalism and political correctness debates. Multiculturalism makes the unfortunate assumption that Akmir is not difficult to deal with. He simply gets added to a list of groups. Political correctness critics respond by saying that they do not want to lengthen the list, their list is fine. What Akmir wants is to do away with lists, or to alter them so as to be unrecognizable to the multiculturalists.

To offer a friendship of play to Akmir is to be forced to find one's own racist patterns of speech and thought. Akmir will see to that. The stories he will tell in Paley's classroom may seem either incomprehensible (in his new language) or belligerent (in the old language) and they will present challenges to the legitimacy of authority. Akmir is not easy to deal with, and yet he must be offered space, space that he can accept.

Kohl concludes the essay by writing that not-learning must be accepted as a strategy rather than dismissed as failure, and that those students who choose to not-learn must be engaged at the level of broad social critique of oppressive institutions (32). Teacher loyalty needs to be directed not toward the system but rather toward the students (32).

The directing of loyalty has been an underlying concern throughout this chapter. For psychoanalysis, loyalty needs to be directed at patients rather than at the analyst or at the history of great figures. Irigaray realizes that the language of psychoanalysis is problematic, just as Akmir realizes that the language of school is problematic. In both cases, the goal is to change the language from one of exclusion to one of inclusion in which friendships of play can be formed even with the "difficult cases."

Derrida finds, in de Man, just such a difficult case. His loyalty to de Man is not blind and stupid, but rather is cautious and thoughtful. Derrida refuses to take the easy way out—to denounce all anti-Semitism as proof that he is not anti-Semitic, that he comprehends the worst of the worst, and will thus not ever be party to it. Comforting to know perhaps, but this is not knowledge that anyone has.

Rather than being loyal to some notion of the history of philosophy as pure intellect free from prejudice, Derrida chooses to be loyal to de Man, to think through the consequences of de Man's work for the history of philosophy. This is not to say that Derrida will not render judgment; rather it is to say that he will reserve judgment for an appropriate time. This time will come through reading and story telling, not through hasty denunciations in op-ed pages of national newspapers.

Akmir and de Man are both difficult cases seemingly on opposite sides of the fence. Akmir challenges the group to stop being racist, de Man presents the group with a secret history of at least questionable merit. In both cases, the group's identity is called into question and the public persona each person projects is called into question. I am not a racist; I have never had an impure thought; I am transparent and good. Valorizing oneself leads to denunciations of others. What is called for is a more honest perception of oneself, and a space from which to speak that honest perception without fear of retribution.

Friendships of play create shame-free (which is not to say shameless) spaces in which secrets can be revealed without fear of retribution, in which dreams can be spoken without fear of ridicule. De Man waited until death to speak his secret and left grieving, shocked friends to do what was partially his work. Likely it is that he had no choice because the institutions would not listen. Akmir had no space in school to dream and this lack of space ultimately pushed him to his death.

The response to such deaths must be willing offers of friend-ship before the crisis has a chance to rise in the distance. *Je ne pveut pas lire/je ne pveut pas entendre/je ne pveut pas écouter* must be replaced by "You can't say you can't play."

Lyotard Revisited

Kohl identifies students whose refusal to play is based on an awareness of the oppressive nature of a given institution. These students refuse the oppression and so refuse to join. Kohl argues that what the group needs to do is to come to see its oppressive structures and change them. But what if the group cannot see? What if it runs smack into a *différend*? Here I want to return to Lyotard whose notion of the *différend* provides an important challenge to the possibility of open play.

As I discussed in the previous chapter, the *différend* is a structural limit on the possibility of communication. My story annihilates you and your story annihilates me and so there is no way we can play together, nor even recognize one another's pres-ence. The logic of the *différend* goes beyond this. Lyotard writes:

> If there is terror in Nazism, it is exerted internally
> among the "pure," who are always suspected of not
> being pure enough. They cleanse themselves of suspi-
> cion by excepting themselves from all impurity
> through oaths, denunciations, pogroms, or final solu-
> tions. This terror does not contain within itself the
> principle of its infinite extension, since it cannot apply
> to what is incapable of being "pure." Jews (and oth-
> ers) are not suspect, they are already judged. (103)

Not only are we busy excluding one another and annihilating
one another, we are also busy with hysterical self-doubt and
self-negation, and this focus on the self begins to take over,
leaving the other to his or her own devices.

The development of the *différend* in this direction helps
explain first why it is that Paley finds one or a few children
excluded year after year, habitually and permanently. The excluded ones are the negation of the "we" and hence the definition
of the "we." The "we" becomes so obsessed with its own purity
and "we"-ness that it cannot allow any connection with the
not-we. Younger children play through this logic with games
like "cooties" in which someone is rendered temporarily impure. Gradually, the impurity sticks to a few kids. In order to
preserve the purity of the "we," no member of the we is to
touch, in any way, one of the others.

The need not to touch combined with hysterical panic
about contagion leads to the constant harassment of the other.
Members of the "we" taunt and tease and test each other through
the forcing of contact and the observing of the response to the
contact. Those in the "we" must be sufficiently "grossed out" in
order to be judged pure. The other cannot simply be left alone—
a better fate than the constant negative attention and tormenting—because the "we" is hysterically obsessed with purity.

Paley's job as a teacher is to keep the we-making fluid
enough that it never hardens into identity-formation. That is,

the stakes of any "we" cannot become so great that terror results. Without one's identity as pure at stake, one has the chance to relax, ease out of the hysterical mode, and enjoy play. Again, Paley notes that the children seem relieved when they no longer have to exclude. This relief may well stem from the chance to stop worrying about their own purity.

This kind of tormenting is not limited to the classroom; it can also be found in the psychoanalytic setting, and it is addressed by Irigaray's refusal to stick to the tradition in psychoanalysis. The analyst who decides that certain symptoms have universal causes harasses his or her patients, returns to certain issues over and over again, and reads all refusals as resistance to the truth rather than as denial of falsity. If the analyst's concern is directed inward at his or her own purity in the face of the tradition, the result is the same tormenting that is found in school. The patient ceases to be in any positive sense and becomes only the negative source of identity for the analyst.

Akmir's high school counselor who refused to grant the diploma on citizenship grounds is also implicated in this logic, as is Akmir himself in his membership in the 7 percent, a Nation of Islam splinter group. The counselor, certain of his own merits and yet hysterically uncertain, denies membership to Akmir as a way of proving his own worth. Even when Akmir seems to have passed the test (taken another class and done well) the counselor refuses to grant the diploma.

Just as the counselor does not want Akmir in the group, so Akmir does not want the counselor. They are mutually negatively defining, mutually exclusive. Akmir's position in society forces him into the oppressed group, and yet to the extent that he can, he refuses to be oppressed. Rather, he redefines the terms and becomes strong.

When faced with a *différend*, one has a variety of choices, which are sometimes made by others and sometimes left up to individuals. One possibility is to accept the terms and live with total self-negation. This dissociating from oneself is perhaps what led Otto Weininger to kill himself because the Nazis, *avant la lettre*, were right. In this instance, one judged as "other" accepts the designation and never hopes for better.

Another choice is to find a substitute. Thus, if one is oppressed economically, one finds a racial or gender equivalent to oppress. These terms are fairly interchangeable in that however one feels oppressed, one can always oppress with regard to one of the other terms. Multiculturalist moves merely add to the list of possible ways to oppress when one is oppressed.

Another choice is to hope that the in group will judge one pure enough to be let in. The person who hopes for this ends up being even more hysterical about purity than does any member of the pure group. Here, J. Edgar Hoover as closeted gay comes to mind, as does the notion of the male-identified woman.

What Akmir does suggests yet another choice—opting out of the system. Had he been less concerned with issues of his own purity and more concerned with the wrong-headedness of purity as a concern, he would have fit this possibility more completely.

The final possibility is offering a friendship of play. It is similar to opting out but not quite the same. To opt out is still to accept the existence of the system because one sees oneself leaving something. What is called for is something a little less rational. If there is a complete denial that there is a fundamentally corrupt social system, and friendship is offered over any and all boundaries, then the boundaries start to lose their power.

This is a place to be careful because I do not want to fall into the "some of my best friends are . . ." game, nor do I want to forget that social boundaries have very real effects on the lives of very real people. What I do want to do is see friendship as a potent political tool, as an opening of private space and as a mirroring of public space.

For friendship to work across the various social boundaries, the friends need to maintain a willful blindness or a spot of irrationality. They must live in denial of boundaries while still seeing the boundaries. The contradictions here are both external and internal. The external contradiction is that even as people know they are not supposed to play with another, they do indeed play, and play in a nonpatronizing way. To play in this manner requires losing sight of the boundaries that make the relationship transgressive. At the same time, though, they need to be aware of the political power and the various political issues that created the boundaries in the first place.

The internal contradictions are likely harder to live with because they concern notions of one's own purity. That is, if someone is taught that associating with someone from this other group will lead to dread diseases, mental impairment, or cooties, then when the association occurs, it causes the fear of impurity. The fear of impurity, in turn, can lead to vicious behavior in an effort to "prove" one's purity while knowing that one is, indeed, impure. Within a friendship, though, the friends need to stop thinking in terms of purity and impurity, even while being reminded regularly that these are issues. One has to accept one's impurity while denying that there is such a thing.

A quick concrete example will help to clarify these issues. Imagine living in a segregated midsize town and having a conversation with a friend about going for a walk or looking for a house to buy. If the friend is in your same social group, then there are clear boundaries for where to walk or where to buy. If your friend is in another social group, then it becomes just about impossible to talk about these basic activities. And yet there is a friendship. Each person must be aware of the boundaries and yet unaware—aware because the boundaries are enforced by others and even by the friends at times ("Oh no, I can't walk there and be safe"; "What do you mean, I do it all the time.") and unaware because they are friends ("Sure I'll go over to your house.").

The writers I have discussed so far nearly all find ways to offer friendship through social boundaries. They all, in one way or another, say "You can't say you can't play." Paley makes sure that not even mutual irritation stops play; Irigaray calls for analysts to stop being loyal to the tradition and to themselves, even at great personal psychic cost; Kohl, a teacher, respects the decision to not-learn. Lyotard's role, here, is less to find prescriptive solutions than it is to provide a description of the structures that bar friendship. And Aristotle's model of friendship provides the tradition against which mine stands.

The final thinker I want to turn to is, once again, Rorty. I want to see how the notion of a friendship of play can augment his discussions of humiliation, irony, and the public/private distinction.

Irony, Cruelty, Rorty

In *Contingency, Irony, Solidarity*, Rorty writes:

The vocabulary of self-creation is necessarily private, unshared, unsuited to argument. The vocabulary of justice is necessarily public and shared, a medium for argumentative exchange. (xiv)

I would argue, however, that self-creation is necessarily private only under a certain conception of what it means to create oneself. If the parricidal strong poet ceases to be the hero of the moment, then self-creation can be seen as a more communal project.

In Paley's classroom, play and story telling are the principal means for self-creation and self-expression, for community making and for setting up a microcosmic just society. Here, self-creation is more than private, though somewhat less than public. By encouraging the children to share in their story making, and by getting them to be more flexible in their decisions, Paley sets up a situation in which the vocabularies of the self and the world meet. My self-creation needs to be just, and justice needs to give me a turn to tell stories; I direct no cruelty to others and no one directs cruelty toward me.

The children are ironists in that they have a sense of the contingency of their stories, but they are not ironists when it comes to "You can't say you can't play" because this rule both constitutes the classroom and guarantees fair play for each child. Perhaps this is their (my) Habermasian or Kantian foundationalist moment about which irony is impermissible.

If this is the case, then the language of the friendship of play is my final vocabulary. Were I ironic about it, then I would have no problem with thinking that things could be different, that friendship is one of many possible responses and it is the one I have chosen for contingent rather than necessary criteria.

If irony goes only this far and no further, then I do not have much of a problem with it. But it does indeed go further in Rorty. Irony is what allows the strong poet to be comfortable humiliating in private, committing parricide at the word processor, and being more concerned with his or her own projects than with the effects of those projects. In a word, irony is one possible precondition of cruelty.

Rorty defends irony on this point by arguing first that metaphysics be cruel, and second by arguing that irony fails to empower, it does not try to humiliate (90–91). He writes:

> The liberal metaphysician wants our *wish to be kind* to be bolstered by an argument, one which entails a self-redescription which will highlight a common human essence, an essence which is something more than our shared ability to suffer humiliation. The liberal ironist just wants our *chances of being kind*, of avoiding the humiliation of others, to be expanded by redescription. (91)

Irony mixed with hope is not really the problem, though. The real tension in Rorty is taking this irony mixed with hope, locking it into the world of private purposes, and adding a dose of romantic strong poet self-creative fervor. He thinks people fault irony for its inherent cruelty, while failing to fault metaphysics for its inherent cruelty. But neither irony nor metaphysics is solely responsible for cruelty. Indeed, it is the desire for the originary that seems to cause most of the trouble. Rorty thinks he has solved this problem by separating the public from the private but, as I have argued, this separation is unstable and untenable.

Post-Rortian philosophy is caught between a rock and a hard place. The rock is the metaphysical certitude that Truth is around the corner and so we can be cruel as we uncover it; and the hard place is the ironic certitude that nothing I think in private has any effect on the world and so I can be as cruel as I want at home when the shades are drawn. Everything important is public for the metaphysician; everything important is private for Rorty. In the ever-sought-after middle is, I would argue, the friendship of play.

Two social practices that I have talked about in this chapter, psychoanalysis and education, are both concerned with redescription. Because Rorty finds it humiliating to accept someone else's redescription of you, he must in some way disallow these two practices. Psychoanalysis is left unmentioned, and education is transmogrified into edification which, for Rorty, is a self-imposed private reading program.

Irigaray, Paley, and Kohl all agree with Rorty that these practices can be humiliating, and indeed often are, but not inherently so. Traditional psychoanalysis with the analyst's needs at the fore is humiliating, traditional classroom exclusions are humiliating, and traditional racist teaching is humiliating. In each case, the humiliation stems not from redescription per se, but from the content of the redescription and from the motivations behind the choice of content.

Analysts and teachers who allow humiliation want it as a tool to control thought and behavior. Irigaray's analysts want to control their own thoughts, and many teachers want to control their students' current and future behavior. The rewards for those in power are clear. Analysts stop being troubled by their own "economy of death," and teachers not only have fewer hassles in the classroom, they also often get praised for having such well-behaved kids. Good behavior that stems from the fear of humiliation is not so good, though.

Within a context of friendship, accepting redescriptions from others is not only not humiliating, it can even be liberating or at least enjoyable. A rape victim in analysis learns to rethink herself as no longer a victim and as no longer identified solely by the rape. A "problem student" in a good classroom learns to channel energy toward a new set of goals and becomes a successful student. In each case, the people in power create a context of care for the other, so that the possibility of humiliation does not arise.

Herbert Kohl's Hebrew school teacher deliberately humiliated him, and most of us have similar experiences. These acts are open, clear, and are not missed by anyone involved. More subtle are the humiliations of exclusive language and reference. As hyper as the political correctness brigade can seem sometimes, people who engage in this practice do indeed unearth phrases, references, and habits of speech that make people feel less than worthy of friendship. It may well be irritating to be a careful speaker in day-to-day discourse, but it is probably worthwhile. In analysis, in the classroom, and in any other situation of power, it is crucial to be a careful speaker.

Rorty, of course, knows that public humiliation is cruel. The problem is that although he relegates humiliation to private space, it will not stay there. And indeed, the more people try to keep things private the more likely they are to feel humiliated about them. It is a common experience to feel relieved after giving voice to a humiliating thought or action. The relief comes from not feeling alone in the knowledge and from feeling that someone can be trusted with one's most vulnerable moments.

If Rorty adopts "You can't say you can't play," what happens to his account? The first thing to go would be the strong poet whose greatest desire is parricide. In place of this figure is a poet whose creations have room for parents, for the tradition, and for change. The strong poet cannot exclude any more than can the classroom bully. But just as Akmir needs space to remake language, so does the strong poet. The key here is that a context of friendship rather than violence must be present. Each side needs to adjust for the other, but neither can desire the annihilation of the other.

Humiliating others is clearly a way of keeping them from playing. If one's psyche does not fit back together after some traumatic moment (torture- or teacher-induced) then one is not going to be able to play. Those who humiliate, those who torture must feel enough distance from the object of their attentions that no fellow feelings are engaged. Within a context of global friendship, presumably torture is less likely to happen. Of course, I cannot say that my account of the world will end torture as we know it along with all the other things I don't like about the world, but it does seem that some of the more awful social practices would be less likely to happen were we to adopt friendship rather than competition as our practice.

Is there room for irony within friendship and about friendship? As I noted earlier, irony that merely says the world could be different is not a problem. But irony, I would argue, can go further and end up saying that since everything is contingent about my friends, I do not care about this particular group of friends, or anything particular for that matter. General irony about truth, does not, in Rorty, stay general. It gets particularized in private moments of self-creation, and thus undermines friendship.

By privileging irony as the outlook to adopt, Rorty makes particularized solidarity (i.e., friendship) problematic. He leaves us with generalized solidarity, which is expressed as "Cruelty is the worst thing we do. Humiliation is the worst form of cruelty. I need to learn more about humiliation."

If Rorty backs away from irony, not to the point of metaphysics, which is not a solution to anything, but rather to the point of an earnest commitment to friends, then it seems to me he would have less trouble with the side effects of irony. Irony is important for Rorty more because it makes room for the strong poet than for what it does to metaphysics. And this is the problem with irony—it opens the way to the cruelty of the desire for the originary.

Solidarity, too, needs some adjustment in Rorty's account. Rather than constituting solidarity negatively, as in, there go some more potential victims of humiliation, Rorty needs a positive account of solidarity. Friendship is clearly one such account. Others are seen not as sufferers, but as joyous additions to life. Aristotle writes that man is a risible animal. To generalize friendship is to generalize laughter and play, clearly a more positive basis for solidarity than is the fear of humiliation.

Notes

•

Chapter 1

1. Judith Robert and Tom Kapacinskas helped explain to me the particulars of bipolar mood disorder.

2. It ought to be admitted here that the analogy falters on this point because infantile regression is considered part of depression and not part of mania.

3. Cf. Rée's "Timely Meditations": "Inevitably he [Rorty] has been greeted as the longed-for peacemaker, a saviour who will release philosophy from its moody exile" (Rée 31).

4. Bencivenga's "Rorty and I" is both amusing and serious in its taking Rorty's "we" personally. Comay also problematizes Rorty's use of "we."

5. Cf. Prado's *The Limits of Pragmatism* in which he argues that Rorty's notion of correspondism is limited to one version of the theory and so Rorty's refutation is equally limited (Prado, 25–37).

6. Nuyen and Caputo argue that Rorty's version of Gadamer and hermeneutics fails to square with Gadamer's texts. Nuyen writes, "Gadamer would object strongly to [Rorty's] characterisation of his hermeneutics as replacing the epistemological project of seeking truth and knowledge" (Nuyen, 70). Caputo writes, "In the end we get from Rorty neither

Heideggerian 'thought' nor Gadamerian 'hermeneutics' " (Caputo, 662).

7. Cf. Goldman's "Rorty's New Myth of the Given" in which he notes that the material conditions Rorty requires for this conversation are problematic (Goldman, 106).

8. Eldridge discusses reading as "apt for the at least partial characterization and expression of something like human nature" (Eldridge, 124). Eldridge's version of reading is one more grounded than is Rorty's, and shows the kind of nostalgia for fixed identity that Rorty argues against.

9. Rée suggests that Rorty's historicism is a limited one given that Rorty limits history to the literary canon and linguistic practice to the discussion of the canon (Rée, 36).

10. I discuss the issue of the genius in Chapters 2 and 4.

Chapter 2

1. Jackson notes that because Rorty wants to be recognized as a philosopher, he must do work that is familiar to philosophers. Familiarity, then, is a criterion for inclusion (Jackson, 385).

2. For Rorty, the way we know our own pain, the problem of privileged access, is precisely the issue he wants to get away from. *How* we know about pain is not interesting for him.

3. Phillips suggests that the way Rorty defines cruelty as exclusive—as being salient for us or not—undermines the "usual force" of the term (Phillips, 366).

4. Rée suggests that Rorty's emphasis on *linguistic* pain as a distinctively human phenomenon is odd to say the least (Rée, 34).

5. Cf. Rorty's discussion of "free discussion" (Rorty 1989, 84).

6. Cf. Fraser's "From Irony to Prophecy to Politics." Fraser argues that for Rorty real innovation is left to "the figure of the feminist as prophet and outcast, the solitary eccentric or mem-

ber of a small embattled separatist club, huddled together spinning a web of words as a charm to keep from going crazy" (Fraser, 263). Fraser's point throughout this essay is that she wants "to put a more sociological, institutional, and collective spin on these ideas and to divest [Rorty's] account of its individualistic, aestheticizing, and depoliticizing residues" (Fraser, 263). Thus, innovation can be public, creation can be non-Oedipal, and feminists need not be prophets.

7. I will return to the idea of thinking the impossible in Chapter 4.

8. On "Rorty's pragmatized Romanticism," Hall writes:

> Art does not reach for the ineffable or the sublime; art lets us get what we want. What we want, above all, is the freedom and imagination to create ourselves in private. A second aim is to avoid behaving cruelly to other people. There are no hard and fast rules to guide us in our attempt responsibly to balance these two aims. (Hall, 40)

I would argue that the absence of rules is caused by the impossibility of the mission.

9. I would like to thank an anonymous reader of part of chapter one for pointing out the importance of cultural belatedness for Rorty.

10. Rée cites Ethel Smyth on "up-to-datism"—our being "in thrall to our times, [so that] we shall not need to think about keeping up with them." (Rée, 39).

Chapter 3

1. Cf. Bontekoe on the difficulties of settling disagreements by appealing to a third vocabulary (Bontekoe, 225–226). Cf. McCumber who argues that we can construct "narrative links among peripatetic economics, the novels of Jane Austen,

and quantum physics. No such links exist, of course, but we invent some. These inventions have no explanatory value" (McCumber, 16). In principle, then, we can construct anything with new vocabularies, but this "anything" is more likely to be useless than to be useful. McCumber adds that such a narrative would be "*interesting*" (McCumber, 17).

2. Cf. Hall's reference to smugness (Hall, 9).

3. Ferrara questions Rorty's "uncritical buying into the liberal assumption of an unbridgeable gap" between the public and private (Ferrara, 93).

4. Nuyen suggests that Rorty's use of freedom is problematic in that it is "too weak and too strong" (Nuyen, 76). It is too weak in that simply multiplying ideas gives us no critical force, and it is too strong in that it is above reproach, or, "is itself beyond criticism" (Nuyen, 76). Bhaskar suggests that the issue of freedom is much more complex than Rorty's account assumes (Bhaskar, 173–174).

Chapter 4

1. Rée suggests that "Rorty's description of the linguistic sadism of the torturer applies to his own treatment of metaphysicians" (Rée, 38). Clearly, Rorty's treatment is public, not private.

2. Cf. Rée's suggestion that Rorty is still "in thrall to Kantian transcendentalism" (Rée, 35). Also cf. Hall's suggestion "that Rorty is overly sanguine about his ability to free himself from Kant, that he remains bound to a quasi-Kantian form of the modernist problematic" (Hall, 53).

3. By "transgression," I mean that which liberates us from obligation, that which sets a limit we are not to cross. But because limits presuppose the beyond, the setting of a limit is also the demarcation of the beyond, and so can act as an invitation to the beyond.

4. We must be aware of the extent to which private fantasy does indeed cross over to public action. Sex fantasies have

a bearing on the practice of sex, and so the private mental space does not long stay mental. Here we see how the private can collapse into the public.

5. In this vein, Kolb writes, "Rorty's divorce of private irony from public tolerance could deny opportunities for internal and dialogic criticism that might exist even without a unified critical project" (Kolb, 144).

6. Rorty continues this discussion in "De Man and the American Cultural Left"—a rewrite of "Two Cheers." And he goes further in "Intellectuals in Politics: Too Far In? Too Far Out?" and in "For a More Banal Politics"—an excerpt from "The Intellectuals at the End of Socialism." In these latter two pieces, Rorty is advocating that intellectuals *do* something—write for *Newsweek*, and talk about "greed."

7. Kant discusses genius in sections 46–50 of the *Critique of Judgment*. Kant writes, "That is why if an author owes a product to his genius, he himself does not know how he came by the ideas for it; nor is it in his power to devise such products by his pleasure . . ." (Kant 1987, 308). And later, "Moreover, the artist's skill cannot be communicated but must be conferred directly on each person by the hand of nature" (Kant 1987, 309).

8. Cf. Weislogel's suggestion that the depoliticization of what really matters to someone leads to "a cynicism and apathy which denigrates the very politics this option was to have liberated" (Weislogel, 310).

9. Cf. Comay.

10. Cf. the discussion in chapter one about Rorty's closet realism.

11. On the issue of elitism, Hall writes:

There is an elitism expressed in Rorty's account. Only a few will be able to pursue the project of self-perfection. The vast majority of individuals in a democratic society will, at best, lead rather insipid lives. Rorty's democratic sentiments . . . are seriously qualified. Democracy is the vehicle for the rise in the minimum standards of life—increased freedom and autonomy. But the freedom is a formal freedom, empty in the sense that only a very few will be able to exercise it in a meaning creating and, therefore, meaningful manner (Hall, 37).

12. That is, claims cannot be legitimated under the logic of *différance* because the conditions for legitimation need their own legitimating conditions. *Différance* continually bumps us to a metalevel; it defers judgment even as it accepts the need for judgment. Hegel's dialectic hopes for resolution, Derrida's *différance* has given up hope.

13. Misgeld writes that for Habermas "the issue is not so much the creation of dialogical communities, rather the institutionalisation of dialogue as a principle in all the relevant dimensions of modern societies" (Misgeld, 271). Presumably, Rorty's private sphere will need to be as open to the principle of dialogue as would be changing the electoral system.

14. Ingram notes that for Habermas, "The chief defect of philosophy of consciousness is its location of the original source of valuation and cognition in an isolated subject, thereby ignoring the significance of communicative interaction" (Ingram, 104). To the extent that Rorty privileges and isolates a person's project of self-creation, Rorty falls prey to this criticism.

15. Cf. Hall's discussion of Habermas, which contains points similar to those I am making (Hall, 146–154).

16. Cf. again Nuyen's contention that Rorty's notion of freedom is both "too strong and too weak" (Nuyen, 76) discussed in chapter 3.

17. Cf. Rée's line that "perhaps [Rorty] is more apriorist than ironist" (Rée, 35).

18. On the Habermas/Lyotard debate, Kolb writes, "There has been an acrimonious debate between Habermas and Lyotard concerning the role of rational agreement. For Habermas, Lyotard's fragmented vision provides no real place for a com-

munity to recollect itself and think critically about its goals and practices" (Kolb, 39). Clearly, Lyotard thinks that the *différend* precludes the possibility of the overarching. On the same topic, Steuermann writes:

> The move to language for both Habermas and Lyotard is a way of answering modernity's challenge. But whereas Habermas has to reduce the scope of his analysis in order to argue that communication is grounded on the possibility of giving reasons in language for the claims we raise in speech, Lyotard's approach to language as strategic games stresses the dimension of language which although rule-governed, is not reducible to rational validation. . . . In other words, where Habermas still relies on a theory of knowledge—now disguised in terms of a linguistic rationality—in order to ground an ethical and a philosophical discourse, Lyotard stresses the need for the invention and creation of new rules. (Steuermann, 113)

What Steuermann shows is that for Lyotard, unlike for Habermas, there is incommensurability that can be overcome locally by the invention of a new language game, but that can never be globally overcome by the discovery of *the* language game.

19. On Lyotard's view of justice, Barron writes:

> Lyotard is concerned to suggest a strategy of "revenge" against the law—that is, any system of prescriptions which purports to regulate conflict with a view to finalizing it. On its way to the "right answer," law inevitably excludes and marginalizes statements which cannot be accommodated within its own tightly drawn parameters, and subordinates every claim concerning the meaning of justice to its own metalanguage. (Barron, 35)

Every language game excludes even as it includes, for Lyotard; thus, there is no possibility for complete justice, because there will always be exclusion, and there will always be unspeakable exclusion.

20. Rée writes, "Still whenever Rorty tries to itemise his "social democratic" beliefs, a raft of conservative prejudices seems to override these left-wing intentions. The evils and pretences of capitalism pass without comment . . ." (Rée, 33).

21. Hall's critique of Rorty's "Grand Narrative" includes a questioning of what Rorty omits from his account. Hall writes, "Finally, I believe it quite significant that Rorty has effectively ignored the economic interpretation of modernity" (Hall, 48). That is, Rorty demarcates modernity with reference to Cartesianism, and not with reference to capitalism.

22. On the Habermas/Derrida debate, Ingram writes:

> Habermas objects to this leveling of logic and rhetoric [in Derrida's deconstructive method], of course, and opposes the reduction of critical and communicative functions to the poetic. Because Derrida aestheticizes language, he underestimates the normative dependence of critical interpretation, cultural transmission, individuation, social integration, and acquisition of knowledge on consensually oriented speech. (Ingram, 91–92)

Bibliography

•

Arcilla, René. "Edification, Conversation, and Narrative: Rortyan Motifs for Philosophy of Education," in *Educational Theory*, Vol. 40, No. 1, Winter 1990, pp. 35–39.

Aristotle. *The Nicomachean Ethics*, David Ross, trans. (New York: Oxford University Press, 1980).

Artaud, Antonin. *The Theater and Its Double*, trans. Mary Caroline Richards (New York: Grove Weidenfield, 1958).

Barron, Anne. "Lyotard and the Problem of Justice," in *Judging Lyotard*, ed., Andrew Benjamin (New York: Routledge, 1992).

Bartky, Sandra Lee. "Feminine Masochism and the Politics of Personal Transformation," in *Femininity and Domination: Studies in the Phenomenology of Oppression* (New York: Routledge, 1990).

Bencivenga, Ermanno. "Rorty and I," in *The Philosophical Forum*, Vol. 24, No. 4, Summer 1993, pp. 307–318.

Bhaskar, Roy. *Reclaiming Reality: A Critical Introduction to Contemporary Philosophy* (New York: Verso, 1989).

Bloom, Harold. *The Anxiety of Influence: A Theory of Poetry* (New York: Oxford University Press, 1973).

Bontekoe, Ron. "Rorty's Pragmatism and the Pursuit of Truth," in *International Philosophical Quarterly*, Vol. 30, No. 2, June 1990, pp. 221–244.

Caputo, John D. "The Thought of Being and the Conversation of Mankind: The Case of Heidegger and Rorty," in *The Review of Metaphysics*, Vol. 36, No. 3, March 1983, pp. 661–685.

Comay, Rebecca. "Interrupting the Conversation: Notes on Rorty," in *Telos: A Quarterly Journal of Critical Thought*, No. 69, Fall 1986, pp. 119–130.

Derrida, Jacques. 1992. *Given Time: 1. Counterfeit Money*, trans. Peggy Kamuf (Chicago: University of Chicago Press, 1992).

———. 1991. "Eating Well, or the Calculation of the Subject: An Interview with Jacques Derrida," trans. Peter Connor and Avital Ronnell, in *Who Comes after the Subject?*, ed., Eduardo Cadava, Peter Connor, and Jean-Luc Nancy (New York: Routledge, 1991).

———. 1989. "Biodegradables: Seven Diary Fragments," trans. Peggy Kamuf, in *Critical Inquiry*, Vol. 15, No. 4, Summer 1989, pp. 812–873.

———. 1988. "Like the Sound of the Sea Deep within a Shell: Paul de Man's War," trans. Peggy Kamuf, in *Critical Inquiry*, Vol. 14, No. 3, Spring 1988, pp. 590–652.

———. 1987. "The Theater of Cruelty and the Closure of Representation," in *Writing and Difference*, trans. Alan Bass (Chicago: The University of Chicago Press, 1987).

Descartes, René. *Meditations on First Philosophy*, trans. Donald Cress (Indianapolis: Hackett Press, 1979).

Eldridge, Richard. "Philosophy and the Achievement of Community: Rorty, Cavell, and Criticism," in *Metaphilosophy*, Vol. 14, No. 2, April 1983, pp. 107–125.

Ferrara, Alessandro. "The Unbearable Seriousness of Irony," in *Philosophy and Social Criticism*, Vol. 16, No. 2, 1990, pp. 81–107.

Foucault, Michel. "What Is an Author?" in *The Foucault Reader*, ed., Paul Rabinow (New York: Pantheon Books, 1984).

Fraser, Nancy. 1991. "From Irony to Prophecy in Politics: A Response to Richard Rorty," in *Michigan Quarterly Review*, Vol. 30, No. 3, Summer 1991, pp. 259–266.

————. 1989. "Solidarity or Singularity? Richard Rorty between Romanticism and Technocracy," in *Unruly Practices: Power, Discourse and Gender in Contemporary Social Theory* (Minneapolis: University of Minnesota Press, 1989).

Goldman, Michael. "Rorty's New Myth of the Given" in *Metaphilosophy*, Vol. 19, No. 2, April 1988, pp. 105–112.

Habermas, Jürgen. 1987a. *The Philosophical Discourse of Modernity: Twelve Lectures*, trans. Frederick Lawrence (Cambridge: MIT Press, 1987).

————. 1987b. "Philosophy as Stand-In and Interpreter," in *After Philosophy: End or Transformation*, eds., Kenneth Baynes, James Bohman, Thomas McCarthy (Cambridge: MIT Press, 1987).

————. 1983. "Modernity—An Incomplete Project," in *The Anti-Aesthetic: Essays on Post-Modern Culture*, ed., Hal Foster (Port Townsend, Washington: Bay Press, 1983).

Hall, David L. *Richard Rorty: Prophet and Poet of the New Pragmatism* (Albany: State University of New York Press, 1994).

Hegel, G. W. F. *Phenomenology of Spirit*, trans., A. V. Miller (New York: Oxford University Press, 1977).

Ingram, David. *Habermas and the Dialectic of Reason* (New Haven: Yale University Press, 1987).

Irigaray, Luce. 1993. *Sexes and Genealogies*, trans., Gillian C. Gill (New York: Columbia University Press, 1993).

————. 1991. "The Poverty of Psychoanalysis," trans. David Macey and Margaret Whitford, in *The Irigaray Reader*, ed., Margaret Whitford (Cambridge: Blackwell, 1991).

—1985. *This Sex which Is Not One*, trans. Catherine Porter and Carolyn Burke (Ithaca: Cornell University Press, 1985).

Jackson, Ronald Lee. "Cultural Imperialism or Benign Relativism? A Putnam-Rorty Debate," in *International Philosophical Quarterly*, Vol. 28, No. 4, December 1988, pp. 383–392.

Kant, Immanuel. 1992. *The Conflict of the Faculties*, trans. Mary Gregor (Lincoln: University of Nebraska Press, 1992).

————. 1987. *Critique of Judgment*, trans. Werner S. Pluher (Indianapolis: Hackett Press, 1987).

Kohl, Herbert. *"I Won't Learn from You" and Other Thoughts on Creative Maladjustment* (New York: The New Press, 1994).

Kolb, David. *Postmodern Sophistications: Philosophy, Architecture, and Tradition* (Chicago: The University of Chicago Press, 1990).

Lovibond, Sabina. "Rorty and Feminism," in *New Left Review*, No. 193, May/June 1992, pp. 56–74.

Lyotard, Jean-François. *The Differend: Phrases in Dispute*, trans. Georges Van Den Abbeele (Minneapolis: University of Minnesota Press, 1988).

McCarthy, Thomas. 1992. "Philosophy and Social Practice: Avoiding the Ethnocentric Predicament," in *Philosophical Interventions in the Unfinished Project of Enlightenment*, eds., Axel Honneth et al. (Cambridge: MIT Press, 1992).

———. 1990. "Private Irony and Public Decency: Richard Rorty's New Pragmatism" in *Critical Inquiry* Vol. 16, No. 2, Winter 1990, pp. 355–370.

McCumber, John. "Reconnecting Rorty: The Situation of Discourse in Richard Rorty's *Contingency, Irony and Solidarity*," in *Diacritics: A Review of Contemporary Criticism*, Summer 1990, pp. 2–19.

Misgeld, Dieter. "Modernity, Democracy and Social Engineering," in *Praxis International*, Vol. 7, Nos. 3–4, Winter 1987–1988, pp. 268–285.

Nuyen, A. T. "Rorty's Hermeneutics and the Problem of Relativism," in *Man and World*, Vol. 25, 1992, pp. 69–78.

Paley, Vivian Gussin. 1990a. *The Boy who Would Be a Helicopter: The Uses of Storytelling in the Classroom* (Cambridge: Harvard University Press, 1990).

———. 1990b. *You Can't Say You Can't Play* (Cambridge: Harvard University Press, 1990).

Phillips, Hollibert E. "The Ironist's Utopia: Can Rorty's Liberal Turnip Bleed," in *International Philosophical Quarterly*, Vol. 32, No. 3, September 1992, pp. 363–368.

Prado, C. G. *The Limits of Pragmatism* (Atlantic Highlands, New Jersey: Humanities Press, 1987).

Rée, Jonathan. "Timely Meditations: Review Essay on Richard Rorty, *Contingency, Irony and Solidarity*," *Radical Philosophy*, 55, Summer 1990, pp. 31–39.

Rorty, Richard. 1993. "Trotsky and the Wild Orchids," in *Wild Orchids and Trotsky: Messages from American Universities*, ed., Mark Edmundson (New York: Penguin, 1993).

———. 1992a. "For a More Banal Politics," in *Harper's Magazine*, May 1992, pp. 16–21; excerpted from "The Intellectuals at the End of Socialism" (originally appearing in *The Yale Review*, Spring 1992).

———. 1992b. "The Pragmatist's Progress," in *Interpretation and Overinterpretation*, ed., Stefan Collini (Cambridge: Cambridge University Press, 1992).

———. 1992c. " 'We Anti-Representationalists,' " Review of Terry Eagleton, *Ideology: An Introduction*, in *Radical Philosophy*, 60, Spring 1992, pp. 40–42.

———. 1991a. "De Man and the American Cultural Left," in *Essays on Heidegger and Others* (Cambridge: Cambridge University Press, 1991).

———. 1991b. "Intellectuals in Politics: Too Far In? Too Far Out?" in *Dissent*, Fall 1991, pp. 453–490.

———. 1991c. *Objectivity, Relativism, and Truth: Philosophical Papers Volume 1* (Cambridge: Cambridge University Press, 1991).

———. 1990a. "An Exchange on Truth, Freedom and Politics: Truth and Freedom: A Reply to Thomas McCarthy," in *Critical Inquiry*, Vol. 16, No. 3, Spring 1990, pp. 633–643.

———. 1990b. "Two Cheers for the Cultural Left" in *South Atlantic Quarterly*, Vol. 89, No. 1, Winter 1990, pp. 227–234.

———. 1989. *Contingency Irony and Solidarity* (Cambridge: Cambridge University Press, 1989).

———. 1987. "Thugs and Theorists: A Reply to Bernstein," in *Political Theory*, Vol. 15, No. 4, 1987, pp. 564–580.

———. 1982. *Consequences of Pragmatism (Essays 1972–1980)* (Minneapolis: University of Minnesota Press, 1982).

————. 1979. *Philosophy and the Mirror of Nature* (Princeton: Princeton University Press, 1979).

Rothleder, Dianne. "The End of Killing, the Law of the Mother, and a Non-Exclusionary Symbolic," in *disclosure* # 5, 1996, pp. 63–73.

Soper, Kate. "Smooth but Fuzzy," Review of Richard Rorty, *Objectivity, Relativism and Truth,* and *Essays on Heidegger and Others,* in *Radical Philosophy,* 60, Spring 1992, pp. 37–39.

Steuermann, Emilia. "Habermas vs. Lyotard: Modernity vs. Postmodernity?" in *Judging Lyotard,* ed., Andrew Benjamin (New York: Routledge, 1992).

Weislogel, Eric. "The Irony of Richard Rorty and the Question of Political Judgment," in *Philosophy Today,* Winter 1990, pp. 303–311.

Whitford, Margaret. *Luce Irigaray: Philosophy in the Feminine* (New York: Routledge, 1991).

Wittgenstein, Ludwig. *Philosophical Investigations,* 3rd. ed., trans., G. E. M. Anscombe (New York: Macmillan Publishing Co., Inc., 1958).

Index

•

159

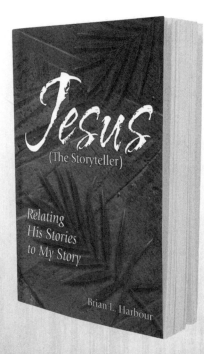
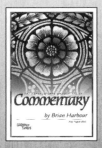

ROADBLOCK #17

When We Feel Sorry for Ourselves
The Self-Pity Roadblock

Search the Scripture
> Psalms 73:16-17; 118:24
> Isaiah 41:10; 59:1
> Matthew 6:34
> Romans 8:18; 8:28; 14:12
> 2 Corinthians 12:10
> Philippians 2:4; 4:19

Our Lessons
> The importance of perspective
> The importance of focus
> The importance of trust

Our Model
> Joseph

Set the Strategy
> Strategy #1: Look at ourselves with a wide-angle lens.
> Strategy #2: Look at God through 3-D glasses.
> Strategy #3: Look at others with x-ray vision.

For more information, see page 129.